Legacy Of Struggle And Resilience: Unearthing The Stories Of Race And Culture

Hagen Laura

Published by Hagen Laura, 2024.

While every precaution has been taken in the preparation of this book, the publisher assumes no responsibility for errors or omissions, or for damages resulting from the use of the information contained herein.

LEGACY OF STRUGGLE AND RESILIENCE: UNEARTHING THE STORIES OF RACE AND CULTURE

First edition. May 17, 2024.

Copyright © 2024 Hagen Laura.

ISBN: 979-8224884544

Written by Hagen Laura.

Table of Contents

Chapter 1: Introduction

DEFINING RACE AND CULTURE

Race and culture are two powerful concepts that shape our understanding of identity and diversity in society. Yet, arriving at a clear and comprehensive definition of these terms can be challenging, as they encompass multifaceted aspects and evolve over time. In this one, we will delve into the nuanced nature of race and culture, exploring how they intersect and influence one another. By examining their historical context, significance, and contemporary understanding, we hope to demystify these concepts and foster a deeper appreciation for the complex tapestry of human experience.

To begin with, let us deconstruct the notion of race. Race is often understood as a social construct, meaning that it is a concept created by society rather than a fixed biological reality. Historically, it has been used to categorize people based on physical characteristics such as skin color, facial features, and hair texture. However, modern scientific research has refuted the idea of discrete racial categories, highlighting instead the genetic similarities and interconnectedness of humanity.

Race operates as a social construct in the sense that it shapes how individuals are perceived and treated within various societies. It influences access to resources, opportunities, and social hierarchies. For instance, the concept of race has played a significant role in the development of systems of oppression such as colonialism, slavery, and apartheid. These systems have perpetuated inequalities based on race, leading to immense suffering and marginalization for certain racial groups throughout history.

Culture, on the other hand, encompasses a broader range of human beliefs, behaviors, values, traditions, and practices. It is often passed down from one generation to another through socialization processes, shaping how individuals perceive the world and interact with others. Culture is not limited to a specific racial or ethnic group; it can be shared across various communities or even transcend national boundaries.

Cultural identities are formed through the intersection of several factors, including language, religion, customs, arts, literature, and cuisine. These elements contribute to a sense of belonging and provide a framework for understanding oneself and others. Culture is not static; it is continually evolving and adapting to new contexts and influences. It is through culture that societies develop unique identities, yet they also interact and exchange ideas with other cultures, enriching their own perspectives.

To fully understand the relationship between race and culture, we must recognize that they are deeply intertwined. Cultural practices often emerge and evolve within specific racial or ethnic groups, reflecting their history, experiences, and values. This connection between race and culture is evident in the diverse array of traditions, celebrations, and artistic expressions found around the world. For example, African American culture in the United States has distinct elements that have emerged from the historical experiences of slavery, segregation, and the Civil Rights Movement.

However, it is important to avoid essentializing cultures or making assumptions about individuals based solely on their racial or ethnic background. This can perpetuate stereotypes and limit our understanding of people's complexities and individuality. All individuals have unique experiences and identities that cannot be reduced to a single racial or cultural attribute.

In today's globalized world, the boundaries between cultures are becoming increasingly blurred, and individuals often navigate multiple cultural identities. This phenomenon, known as multiculturalism or hybridity, challenges traditional notions of culture as static and homogeneous. It highlights the fluid and dynamic nature of cultural practices and identities, as individuals blend elements from various cultures to form their own unique expressions.

While race and culture are intertwined, it is crucial to distinguish between them to avoid essentialism and promote inclusivity. Culture is a dynamic, multifaceted concept that encapsulates a range of human experiences, whereas race is a social construct that has historically been used to create hierarchies and divisions. By recognizing this distinction, we can appreciate the richness and diversity of cultural expressions while challenging oppressive systems that perpetuate racial inequalities. Race is a social construct that has historically been used to categorize individuals based on physical characteristics, while culture encompasses the beliefs, behaviors, and practices of individuals within a community. These concepts intersect in ways that reflect historical experiences, shape identity, and influence societal dynamics. Understanding the intricacies of race and culture is essential to promoting inclusivity, challenging stereotypes, and embracing the diversity of human experiences. By continuously questioning and reevaluating these concepts, we can work towards a more equitable and compassionate society.

Historical Perspectives on Race and Culture

To begin our journey into history, it is important to acknowledge that race and culture are intertwined concepts that have significantly influenced human societies. While race refers to the biological differences between individuals, culture encompasses the beliefs, customs, and practices that shape a group's identity. Throughout history, societies have grappled with navigating the complex interactions between these two aspects of human identity and the consequences of these interactions.

One historical perspective worth examining is the concept of scientific racism, which gained prominence in the late 18th and early 19th centuries. Influenced by the emerging field of anthropology, proponents of scientific racism sought to justify racial hierarchies and discrimination through pseudo-scientific claims. Scholars such as Carl Linnaeus and Johann Blumenbach classified humans into distinct races, often positioning Europeans as superior to other racial groups. These ideas perpetuated the belief in inherent racial superiority or inferiority, leading to the justification of colonization, slavery, and other forms of systemic oppression.

However, it is important to note that historical perspectives on race and culture are not solely characterized by discrimination and dominance. The history of civil rights movements in different parts of the world provides evidence of resistance and the fight against racial and cultural oppression. For example, in the United States, the Civil Rights Movement of the 20th century led to significant advancements in racial equality, challenging long-standing discriminatory practices and advocating for social justice.

Furthermore, historical perspectives on race and culture shed light on the role of individuals who have shaped the discourse on these topics. Figures such as W.E.B. Du Bois, Frantz Fanon, and Martin Luther King Jr. have played pivotal roles in advocating for racial equality and challenging prevailing social norms. Their contributions have not only advanced the cause of civil rights but have also inspired future generations to work towards a more inclusive society.

Another crucial aspect in understanding historical perspectives on race and culture is examining the impact of colonialism and imperialism. The colonization of different regions by European powers introduced a complex power dynamic that shaped notions of race and culture. European empires imposed their values, norms, and cultural practices upon colonized peoples, often leading to the erasure or marginalization of indigenous cultures. This legacy continues to influence contemporary discussions on decolonization, cultural appropriation, and the need to restore and recognize indigenous knowledge and practices.

Moreover, historical perspectives on race and culture highlight the influence of ideologies such as eugenics and nationalism. These ideologies often intersected and reinforced each other, promoting racial purity and the superiority of a specific culture. Eugenic policies, which sought to control reproduction based on perceived genetic fitness, were implemented in various countries, leading to forced sterilizations and other human rights violations. Nationalism, on the other hand, created a fervent loyalty to one's own culture or nation, often at the expense of minority groups. Understanding the historical roots of these ideologies is crucial in recognizing their impact and advocating for an inclusive and diverse society. By exploring key events, individuals, and ideologies, we gain a holistic understanding of the complex dynamics that have shaped our world. This knowledge empowers us to challenge discriminatory practices, fight for social justice, and foster a more inclusive and equitable future.

Chapter 2: The Legacy of Colonialism

IMPACT OF COLONIALISM on Race and Culture

One of the most profound impacts of colonialism on race is the creation and perpetuation of racial hierarchies. European colonial powers, such as the British, French, Spanish, and Portuguese, imposed their own racial classifications on the indigenous peoples they encountered in their colonies. These classifications were often based on physical characteristics, such as skin color and facial features, and were used to justify and institutionalize discriminatory practices. Ignoring the diverse ethnicities and cultures that existed within colonized territories, colonial powers labeled indigenous peoples as inferior and subjugated them to various forms of exploitation and marginalization.

Furthermore, colonialism played a pivotal role in the construction and consolidation of white supremacy, both at the individual and structural level. The colonizers, primarily of European descent, considered themselves racially superior to the indigenous populations and used this perceived superiority to legitimize their dominance and control. This sense of racial superiority was deeply ingrained in colonial institutions, laws, and policies, leading to the subjugation and marginalization of non-white populations. The legacy of this racial hierarchy can still be seen today in many former colonies, where racial discrimination and inequalities persist.

In addition to shaping racial dynamics, colonialism also had a profound impact on culture. Colonial powers sought to impose their own cultural values and norms on the colonized peoples, often through systems of education, religion, and language. The goal of cultural assimilation was to create a sense of homogeneity and facilitate control by erasing or marginalizing indigenous cultures and practices. For instance, colonial powers often promoted their own languages and discouraged the use of indigenous languages, relegating them to the status of inferiority. Similarly, the imposition of Eurocentric education systems often undermined indigenous knowledge and contributed to a loss of cultural identity.

However, it is important to note that the impact of colonialism on culture was not entirely negative or one-sided. While colonial powers did seek to erase or marginalize indigenous cultures, they also unintentionally facilitated cultural exchange and hybridization. The forced interaction between colonizers and colonized people led to the merging and blending of cultural practices, traditions, and even artistic styles. This cultural syncretism has given rise to unique forms of expression that reflect the diverse histories and experiences of formerly colonized populations.

Furthermore, the resistance movements that emerged in response to colonialism played a crucial role in preserving and revitalizing indigenous cultures. These movements, characterized by acts of defiance, cultural pride, and demands for self-determination, worked to reclaim and revalorize indigenous languages, traditions, and knowledge systems. They sought to challenge the dominant narratives imposed by colonial powers and reclaim agency over cultural identities. Today, many former colonies celebrate their cultural heritage and take pride in their resilience against the forces of colonization. It has contributed to the creation and perpetuation of racial hierarchies, both at the individual and structural level, while also influencing cultural dynamics through processes of assimilation and resistance. Recognizing and understanding these legacies is essential for addressing ongoing racial injustices and promoting greater inclusivity and cultural diversity. By acknowledging the historical roots of contemporary inequalities and celebrating the resilience of formerly colonized peoples, we can work towards a future that values and respects all cultures and races.

Resilience of Indigenous Peoples

This profound resilience stems from their deep-rooted connection to their land, rich cultural heritage, and collective spirit. In this one, we will explore the multifaceted dimensions of resilience among indigenous communities, shedding light on the challenges they have faced and the strategies they have developed to navigate adversity. By examining the historical context and contemporary realities, we aim to celebrate the resilience of these communities while advocating for their rights and promoting sustainable development that respects their unique worldviews and contributions.

Historical Perspectives:

To truly understand the resilience of indigenous peoples, we must first acknowledge the historical traumas they have endured. From colonization and forced assimilation to displacement and marginalization, the history of indigenous communities is marked by significant trauma. However, despite these attempts to undermine their cultural and social fabric, indigenous peoples have consistently demonstrated their resilience by preserving their languages, traditions, and spiritual practices. The strength drawn from their collective identities and deep-rooted connections to ancestral lands has enabled them to endure and thrive amidst immense hardship.

Land as the Foundation:

The intimate relationship between indigenous peoples and their land is a cornerstone of their resilience. For indigenous communities, the land not only provides sustenance but also embodies a spiritual and cultural significance that has shaped their identities for generations. Maintaining their connection to the land not only ensures their physical survival but also allows them to reinforce their cultural practices and intergenerational knowledge. Therefore, efforts to preserve indigenous resilience must center on land rights, recognizing that their ability to govern and protect their territories is vital for maintaining their resilience and self-determination.

Indigenous Knowledge and Wisdom:

Another aspect that contributes to the resilience of indigenous communities is their rich traditional knowledge systems. Indigenous knowledge encompasses a holistic understanding of ecosystems, sustainable resource management practices, and spiritual beliefs deeply rooted in reciprocal relationships with nature. This wisdom, passed down through generations, offers valuable insights into mitigating environmental degradation and promoting sustainable development. By respecting and integrating indigenous knowledge into policymaking and development processes, resilience can be further enhanced, creating harmonious and equitable societies.

Social Empowerment and Cultural Revitalization:

Resilience is not solely about survival; it also involves empowerment and cultural revitalization. Many indigenous peoples have impressively reclaimed and revitalized their cultural practices, languages, and traditional governance structures. Cultural revitalization initiatives have not only strengthened their collective identity but have also empowered individuals and communities to actively participate in decision-making processes. By fostering cultural pride and intergenerational exchange, indigenous communities can tackle challenges more effectively and chart their own paths towards sustainable development.

Strength in Unity:

The resilience of indigenous peoples is deeply embedded in their strong community networks and interdependence. The collective spirit and solidarity within indigenous communities have been instrumental in overcoming challenges. The communal support systems and traditional governance practices that prioritize consensus-building contribute to their resilience. Recognizing and respecting their self-governing structures and fostering partnerships based on trust and respect are essential for supporting indigenous peoples in their resilience journey.

Preserving Indigenous Resilience in the Face of Modern Challenges:

While indigenous peoples have demonstrated remarkable resilience throughout history, they continue to face contemporary challenges that threaten their well-being and cultural survival. Issues such as land encroachment, resource extraction, climate change, and systemic discrimination persist. Therefore, it is crucial to address these challenges by embracing a human rights-based approach, empowering indigenous voices in decision-making processes, and establishing policies that promote their self-determination, cultural preservation, and sustainable development.

THE RESILIENCE OF INDIGENOUS peoples is a testament to the strength of their collective identity, deep connection to their land, and rich cultural heritage. Their ability to endure historical injustices and navigate contemporary challenges provides valuable lessons for societies worldwide. By recognizing and honoring indigenous rights, preserving their traditional knowledge, and fostering inclusive partnerships, we can lay the foundation for a more resilient, diverse, and sustainable future in which indigenous communities can thrive. It is our collective responsibility to ensure that their unique contributions are cherished and integrated into our shared global journey towards resilience.

Chapter 3: Slavery and Its Aftermath

EFFECTS OF SLAVERY on Race Relations

The enduring impact of this deplorable practice on race relations cannot be understated. In order to truly understand the present state of racial dynamics, it is crucial to dive deep into the effects of slavery. This one seeks to shed light on the far-reaching consequences of slavery on race relations, exploring its social, economic, psychological, and political implications. By unraveling this complex web of history, we can foster a more comprehensive dialogue aimed at achieving equality and justice for all.

Slavery's Lingering Legacy:

Unquestionably, slavery has left an indelible legacy on race relations. One of the most palpable effects is the perpetuation of racial stereotypes and biases. Plantation owners and slaveholders propagated demeaning narratives to justify their immoral actions. These narratives, constructed to dehumanize enslaved individuals, persistently shaped public opinion, further entrenching racial discrimination. Deep-rooted prejudices developed during this era continue to permeate our society, creating barriers to genuine social cohesion and inclusivity.

Moreover, the economic implications of slavery on race relations remain evident to this day. Slavery contributed significantly to the accumulation of wealth in the hands of a few, perpetuating socio-economic disparities between different racial groups. Vital resources, such as land and education, were disproportionately allocated, ensuring that descendants of enslaved individuals would face systemic disadvantages. This systemic disadvantage continues to hinder the prospects of economic mobility, leading to ongoing disparities in income, employment, and access to quality education.

Unpacking Psychological Trauma:

The psychological impact of slavery on both enslaved individuals and their descendants is a crucial aspect to consider when examining the repercussions for race relations. Enslaved Africans were subjected to unimaginable brutality, dehumanization, and the complete eradication of their agency. This trauma inflicted deep emotional scars that were passed down through generations. Understanding this intergenerational trauma is vital for comprehending the complexities of contemporary race relations.

Factors such as internalized racism, racial self-hatred, and hypervigilance arose from the systematic degradation suffered by enslaved individuals. These psychological wounds have led to a subconscious perpetuation of racial biases within marginalized communities. Diminishing the impact of slavery on race relations requires a compassionate recognition of these historical traumas and developing healing processes that can restore dignity and self-esteem to individuals and communities disproportionately affected.

Shaping Political Structures and Doctrine:

An examination of the effects of slavery on race relations must also delve into the political realm. The United States, for example, grapples with a legacy deeply rooted in the era of slavery, as evidenced by the enduring struggles for racial equality. Political structures and doctrines entrenched during this time have proven resistant to change, impeding the progress towards true racial justice.

Slavery provided the framework for segregationist policies and discriminatory legislation that persisted long after its abolition. The Jim Crow era, with its overtly racist legislation and virulent systemic oppression, highlighted the tenacious endurance of racial discrimination. This history lingers in contemporary society, albeit in subtler forms. Understanding the political systems motivated by and designed to maintain racial hierarchies is essential for dismantling and rebuilding equitable institutions that promote genuine racial reconciliation.

Looking Ahead: Toward a Path of Racial Equality:

Recognizing the historical imprint of slavery on race relations equips us with the knowledge and perspective required to forge a more inclusive future. To pave the path towards racial equality, we must engage in active dialogue, education, and introspection. It is our collective responsibility to confront and challenge the prejudices we have inherited, consciously striving to promote inclusivity and equity for all.

By raising awareness of the enduring consequences of slavery, we foster a society that embraces diversity and dismantles the oppressive systems that still pervade many aspects of our world. Through policy changes, educational efforts, and genuine empathy, we can forge a path toward racial healing, unity, and social harmony.

THE EFFECTS OF SLAVERY on race relations have left an indelible mark on our society. This one has aimed to illuminate the varied and far-reaching implications, spanning social, economic, psychological, and political realms. Acknowledging the ongoing impact of slavery fosters a deeper understanding of the disparities experienced by marginalized groups today.

While the heritage of slavery continues to create challenges, it is not insurmountable. By cultivating a compassionate and informed approach to race relations, we can strive for justice, equality, and a society where the sins of our past do not dictate the course of our future. It is a collective responsibility to dismantle the systemic barriers that perpetuate racial discrimination and to pave the way for a more equitable world for all.

Cultural Resistance among Enslaved Populations

Trapped in a system that sought to strip them of their humanity and cultural identity, enslaved populations worldwide demonstrated remarkable resilience and developed unique methods of resistance. This essay delves into the concept of cultural resistance among enslaved populations, exploring the various forms it took and its enduring impact on the empowerment and preservation of cultural identity.

Preserving Cultural Identity:

Enslaved individuals faced a relentless assault on their cultural identity, as their oppressors aimed to erase any connections to their native cultures. Despite these attempts, enslaved populations fiercely held on to their inherent cultural traditions, passed down from generation to generation. Music, dance, art, language, and spiritual practices became crucial avenues for expressing their shared African identity and resisting the dehumanizing effects of enslavement. This intentional preservation of cultural practices became a powerful shield against assimilation and a source of empowerment, instilling a sense of dignity and pride within enslaved populations.

Forms of Cultural Resistance:

In the face of adversity, the enslaved developed a myriad of forms of cultural resistance that covertly challenged the dominant power structures. One of the most prominent manifestations can be seen in the creation of cultural expressions such as music and dance. These art forms not only served as a means of entertainment but also allowed enslaved individuals to celebrate their heritage, communicate with each other, and subtly challenge the oppressive systems in which they existed.

Musical resistance, exemplified by chants, spirituals, and rhythms, presented a form of communal expression that provided solace, conveyed coded communication, and often expressed desires for freedom. The powerful rhythm and message of songs like "Wade in the Water" or "Go Down Moses" not only lifted spirits but also contained secret messages about escape routes and plans. Dance movements, similarly, became a venue for both personal and collective empowerment, providing enslaved populations a sense of freedom and release from their physical constraints.

Another form of cultural resistance emerged through religious and spiritual practices. Enslaved individuals, often forced into practicing Christianity, infused their African spiritual beliefs and practices within the newly imposed religion. By blending elements of African spirituality with Christianity, they created a unique and empowering form of worship. These syncretic practices became a sanctuary for enslaved populations, allowing them to maintain connections with their ancestral beliefs, find solace, and strengthen communal bonds.

Cultural resistance also extended to language, enabling enslaved populations to develop a unique dialect or creole that became a form of resistance and subversion. By creating a distinct language, such as Gullah in the southern United States or Pidgin English in the Caribbean, enslaved individuals could communicate covertly and solidify community bonds. This linguistic resistance allowed them to preserve their cultural heritage, share stories, and maintain a sense of identity, even amidst severe oppression.

Legacy of Empowerment:

The legacy of cultural resistance among enslaved populations is both profound and enduring, as it continues to shape contemporary cultural practices and narratives today. Despite attempting to strip away the humanity and cultural identity of enslaved populations, their resistance laid the foundation for the ongoing preservation and celebration of African cultural heritage worldwide.

Cultural resistance contributed to the eventual abolition of slavery, as it challenged dominant narratives and fostered empathy among those outside the enslaved community. The music, art, and stories borne out of this resistance deeply touched the hearts and minds of abolitionists, compelling them to advocate for change and work towards the emancipation of enslaved populations. The resilience and cultural resistance of the enslaved continue to inspire upcoming generations to fight against various forms of oppression, striving for social justice and equality.

CULTURAL RESISTANCE among enslaved populations embodied the unwavering spirit to preserve dignity and heritage under the most oppressive conditions. By holding onto their cultural traditions, languages, music, dance, and spiritual practices, the enslaved forged a path of empowerment that defied their oppressors. The enduring legacy of cultural resistance serves as a testament to the power of human resilience and the importance of preserving cultural identity. Understanding and celebrating the resistance of enslaved populations ensures that their stories are never forgotten, promoting inclusivity and inspiring us to dismantle modern-day systems of oppression.

15

Chapter 4: Civil Rights Movement

STRUGGLES FOR RACIAL Equality

Rooted in a long legacy of discrimination, oppression, and systemic inequalities, this topic continues to be of paramount importance in contemporary society. This comprehensive exploration aims to shed light on the struggles faced by marginalized racial and ethnic groups in their relentless pursuit of equality. By closely examining historical contexts, pivotal events, social movements, and the continued challenges faced today, we aim to foster a better understanding of the multifaceted tapestry that is the struggle for racial equality.

Foundations of Struggle

The struggle for racial equality is rooted in a dark history marred by slavery, colonization, and exploitation. This one delves deep into the historical dynamics that set the stage for subsequent struggles. By exploring the origins of racial discrimination and the roots of institutionalized racism, readers will gain an understanding of the deep-seated issues that continue to plague societies today. Special emphasis will be placed on significant historical milestones, such as the abolitionist movement, the transatlantic slave trade, and the civil rights era, which paved the way for future advancements towards racial justice.

Key Movements and Figures

In this one, we explore the influential social movements, individuals, and groups who played pivotal roles in the pursuit of racial equality. From Martin Luther King Jr. and Rosa Parks in the United States to Nelson Mandela in South Africa, various figures and their ideologies are examined in uplifting and engaging detail. By highlighting the tireless efforts of these leaders, community organizers, and everyday activists, readers will gain inspiration and insights into the complex web of struggles for racial equality across the globe.

Education as a Catalyst for Change

Education has always been a powerful tool in the fight against racial inequality. This one examines how educational institutions have both perpetuated and challenged racial disparities, providing a nuanced perspective on their role in shaping societal attitudes. From landmark court cases like Brown v. Board of Education in the United States to the establishment of Black Studies programs, we explore the ways in which marginalized communities have fought for educational equity. Moreover, the one discusses the importance of diverse curriculum, representation, and access to quality education as means to create a more just and inclusive society.

Systemic Racism and Institutional Bias

One of the greatest obstacles to racial equality stems from systemic racism and institutional biases deeply embedded in social structures. By delving into the various systems that perpetuate racial inequities, this one seeks to provide readers with a comprehensive understanding of the broader framework within which struggles for racial equality take place. Exploring systemic issues such as mass incarceration, racial profiling, and housing discrimination, we aim to raise awareness about the multifaceted nature of racial inequality and the importance of dismantling these deeply ingrained systems.

Contemporary Challenges and Moving Forward

Despite significant advancements, our contemporary society continues to grapple with racial inequalities. This one addresses the various challenges faced today, including the resurgence of white supremacy movements, microaggressions, and ongoing socioeconomic disparities. Highlighting recent social justice movements such as Black Lives Matter, readers will gain insights into the ways in which marginalized communities continue to push for equality and advocate for lasting change.

IN CLOSING, THE STRUGGLE for racial equality is an ongoing battle that requires continuous examination and proactive engagement from all members of society. By exploring the historical foundations, key movements, educational challenges, systemic racism, and contemporary obstacles in this comprehensive exploration, we aim to foster an understanding of the complexities surrounding this crucial issue. Through knowledge and empathy, we can collectively work towards building a more just and inclusive society for all.

Chapter 5: Immigration and Assimilation

CHALLENGES FACED BY Immigrant Communities

Immigration is a deeply ingrained part of human history, with countless individuals moving to new lands in search of better opportunities, safety, or new beginnings. The challenges faced by immigrant communities have persisted throughout time, and they continue to impact societies across the globe. In this book, we delve into the multifaceted challenges experienced by immigrant communities, seeking to shed light on their struggles and explore potential solutions. By understanding and addressing these challenges, we can work towards creating a more inclusive and harmonious society for all.

Cultural Adjustment and Integration

One of the most significant challenges faced by immigrant communities is cultural adjustment and integration. Immigrants often find themselves immersed in a new culture, with different values, customs, and social norms. This process of assimilating into a new culture can be both exciting and overwhelming. Language barriers can further complicate matters, as communication is vital for integration and creating meaningful connections within the community. These challenges can lead to feelings of isolation, misunderstanding, and even discrimination, hindering the ability of immigrants to fully participate and contribute to society.

Education and Language Barriers

Education plays a crucial role in the integration and success of immigrant communities, but it is not without its challenges. Language barriers can serve as significant hurdles for immigrant students, impeding their ability to fully comprehend and participate in the educational system. Even with language support programs in place, resources and funding constraints often limit their effectiveness. Additionally, cultural differences may impact the student-teacher relationship and lead to misunderstandings. Schools and educational institutions must prioritize the provision of high-quality language support and culturally responsive education to ensure equal opportunities for all students, regardless of their background.

Access to Healthcare

Access to healthcare is another crucial challenge faced by immigrant communities. Language barriers, unfamiliarity with the healthcare system, and a lack of culturally appropriate services can create a significant gap in healthcare provision. Immigrants may face challenges in understanding their rights, navigating the healthcare system, and finding healthcare professionals who can effectively communicate with them. This can result in delayed or inadequate care, exacerbating health disparities within the immigrant community. A comprehensive approach is needed, addressing linguistic and cultural barriers, improving accessibility, and promoting health literacy to ensure that immigrant communities have equal access to quality healthcare.

Economic Integration and Employment Opportunities

Securing stable employment and achieving economic integration is often a primary goal for immigrant communities. However, numerous barriers can hinder their path to economic success. Discrimination, limited recognition of foreign qualifications, and unfamiliarity with the job market and networking opportunities can all pose significant challenges. Immigrants may also face exploitation in the form of unfair wages or poor working conditions. Moreover, those who belong to marginalized groups within immigrant communities may face additional obstacles due to intersectional discrimination. By addressing these challenges, ensuring equal employment opportunities, and providing support for skill development and recognition, we can empower immigrant communities to thrive economically.

Social Exclusion and Xenophobia

Social exclusion and xenophobia are formidable challenges that immigrant communities often face. Despite the immense contributions immigrants make to society, negative stereotypes and prejudices can foster discrimination and hostility. This can result in social exclusion, limited social interactions, and a sense of marginalization within the larger community. Immigrants must be welcomed and embraced as valuable members of society, with efforts focused on promoting cultural understanding, fostering inclusive communities, and combating stereotypes. Empathy, education, and advocacy play pivotal roles in addressing this challenge and fostering a more inclusive society for all.

Legal and Policy Issues

Legal and policy issues can significantly impact immigrant communities, determining their rights, protections, and opportunities. Immigration policies often change over time, creating uncertainty and anxiety within immigrant communities. Challenges may arise in obtaining legal status, accessing social benefits, or reuniting with family members. Policies that fail to prioritize family unity and fail to provide clear pathways to legal status can create immense hardship and hinder the integration of immigrant communities. Striving for comprehensive immigration reform and sustainable policies that prioritize human rights and dignity is crucial for addressing these challenges.

Community Support and Empowerment

Community support and empowerment are essential components in overcoming the challenges faced by immigrant communities. Building support networks, both within the immigrant community and among the host society, can provide a source of strength, resources, and guidance. Community organizations, non-governmental organizations, and grassroots initiatives play vital roles in providing services and advocating for the rights of immigrants. Empowering immigrant communities involves promoting leadership, civic engagement, and active participation in decision-making processes. By nurturing a sense of belonging, we can help create a more inclusive society that celebrates diversity.

THE CHALLENGES FACED by immigrant communities are complex and multifaceted. From cultural adjustment and integration to education, healthcare, employment, social exclusion, legal issues, and community support, addressing these challenges requires collective effort and commitment. Through policy reform, advocacy, education, and compassion, we can create an environment that supports and empowers immigrant communities. By recognizing and valuing the incredible contributions immigrants make to society, we can build a future that is characterized by inclusivity, respect, and social cohesion.

Preserving Cultural Identity in a New Land

In today's interconnected and globalized world, people from various backgrounds are immigrating to new lands in search of opportunities and a better life. However, the process of adaptation and assimilation into a new culture can pose significant challenges to individuals and communities alike. One crucial aspect of this adaptation process is the preservation of one's cultural identity. This topic holds immense relevance in the modern era, as cultural diversity and inclusivity are increasingly valued and celebrated. In this book, I aim to delve deep into the strategies and approaches individuals and communities can employ to preserve their cultural identity while navigating a new land.

To begin our exploration, it is vital to first understand the concept of cultural identity. Cultural identity is multifaceted and encompasses various elements, including language, customs, traditions, values, and beliefs. These aspects not only shape who we are as individuals but also connect us to a larger community and provide a sense of belonging. When individuals and communities migrate to a new land, they often face the dilemma of balancing their desire to integrate into the new culture with the need to preserve their unique cultural identity. This delicate balance is crucial for maintaining a sense of identity, self-esteem, and cohesion among migrants.

One key strategy for preserving cultural identity in a new land lies in maintaining and celebrating language and communication. Language is the foundation of any culture and serves as a link between generations and communities. Encouraging the continued use of one's native language enables individuals to express themselves authentically and remain connected to their cultural roots. Community organizations, schools, and cultural centers can play instrumental roles in offering language programs and resources to ensure the preservation of linguistic diversity.

Another essential aspect of preserving cultural identity is the celebration and preservation of customs and traditions. Rituals, festivals, and traditional practices are vital expressions of a community's cultural heritage. These events not only provide a platform for showcasing cultural pride but also serve as opportunities for individuals to learn and engage with their own roots. Migrant communities can organize cultural festivals, food fairs, or performances in collaboration with local organizations, fostering cultural exchange and understanding. These events not only preserve cultural traditions but also contribute to the multicultural fabric of the larger society.

Education plays a fundamental role in preserving cultural identity. As migrants settle in a new land, it is essential to maintain a solid connection with their culture of origin. Incorporating cultural education into school curricula, community programs, and extracurricular activities can provide opportunities for individuals, particularly children and young adults, to learn about their cultural heritage. By promoting cultural education, schools foster understanding, respect, and empathy among students from different backgrounds, while simultaneously nurturing a sense of belonging and identity among those from migrant communities.

Recognizing and supporting cultural institutions and organizations is another key strategy for preserving cultural identity in a new land. These organizations serve as hubs for community engagement, fostering a sense of unity and cultural pride. Governments, both local and national, can provide funding and resources to support the establishment and maintenance of cultural centers, museums, libraries, and community spaces dedicated to preserving and promoting diverse cultural traditions. Additionally, individuals and communities can contribute by actively participating in these organizations, supporting cultural initiatives, and sharing their stories and experiences.

As we explore the preservation of cultural identity in a new land, it is important to acknowledge that cultural identities are not fixed or stagnant. They evolve and adapt over time, influenced by new experiences and interactions. Thus, it is crucial to strike a balance between preserving cultural identity and embracing the new cultural landscape. Migrants should be encouraged to take part in the cultural practices of their new home while retaining their traditional customs and traditions. This dynamic interplay between cultures enriches both the individual and the broader society, leading to a more inclusive and diverse community. By maintaining and celebrating language, customs, traditions, and values, individuals and communities can nurture their sense of identity, foster social cohesion, and contribute to the cultural enrichment of their adopted country. Through language programs, cultural events, educational initiatives, and support for cultural institutions, we can ensure that cultural diversity thrives, creating a more inclusive and harmonious society where everyone feels valued and respected.

Chapter 6: Discrimination and Inequality

EFFORTS TO COMBAT DISCRIMINATION

Discrimination has been a pervasive problem throughout human history, but in recent decades, there has been a substantial increase in efforts to combat discrimination in various spheres of society. These efforts have been driven by a growing recognition of the negative impact discrimination has on individuals and communities, as well as a realization that it undermines the principles of equality and fairness that are fundamental to a just and inclusive society. In this one, we will explore some of the key strategies and initiatives that have been employed to combat discrimination, examining both their successes and challenges.

One of the most significant efforts to combat discrimination has been the enactment and enforcement of laws that protect individuals from discrimination based on various grounds such as race, gender, religion, disability, and sexual orientation. These laws aim to create a legal framework that promotes equality and prohibits discriminatory practices in housing, employment, education, and other areas of public life. They provide individuals with a means to seek legal remedies if they have been victims of discrimination and serve as a deterrent for discriminatory behavior.

Another important strategy in combating discrimination is raising awareness and promoting education about the harmful effects of discrimination. Education plays a crucial role in challenging prejudice and stereotypes, promoting empathy and understanding, and fostering a culture of inclusivity. Efforts to combat discrimination in this regard include school curricula that teach about the history of discrimination, the importance of equality, and the value of diversity, as well as awareness campaigns in workplaces and communities that promote tolerance and respect.

Furthermore, organizations and institutions have taken proactive steps to combat discrimination by implementing policies and practices that promote diversity and inclusion. Such initiatives aim to create environments that embrace individuals from all backgrounds and provide equal opportunities for personal and professional development, regardless of one's race, ethnicity, gender, or other characteristics. This may involve measures such as implementing affirmative action programs to address historical disadvantages faced by marginalized communities, establishing mentorship or sponsorship programs to support underrepresented groups, and ensuring unbiased and inclusive recruitment and promotion processes.

In addition to these more formal strategies, grassroots movements and social activism have played a significant role in raising awareness about discrimination and pushing for change. Activists and advocacy groups have mobilized communities, organized protests, and used social media platforms to shine a spotlight on discriminatory practices and demand accountability. These efforts have often led to important policy reforms and changes in public attitudes towards discrimination, with many successful campaigns contributing to the advancement of marginalized groups' rights.

However, despite these commendable efforts, combating discrimination remains an ongoing challenge. Discrimination is deeply ingrained in social structures and institutions, and its manifestations can be subtle and insidious. Moreover, progress in combating discrimination can sometimes be slow and hindered by resistance or backlash from those who benefit from or actively perpetuate discriminatory practices. It is, therefore, crucial that efforts to combat discrimination remain vigilant, adaptive, and inclusive of diverse perspectives.

Additionally, it is important to recognize the intersectionality of discrimination and acknowledge that individuals often face multiple forms of discrimination based on various intersecting aspects of their identity. Efforts to combat discrimination must, therefore, take into account the complex ways in which various forms of marginalization can interact and multiply the negative impacts on individuals. Intersectional approaches to combating discrimination prioritize the experiences and needs of those most marginalized to ensure that efforts to combat discrimination are genuinely inclusive and address the root causes of inequality. These efforts have taken the form of legal protections, educational initiatives, institutional policies, grassroots movements, and social activism. While progress has been made, discrimination remains a persistent challenge, requiring ongoing commitment and adaptation. By continuing to raise awareness, fostering inclusive environments, and recognizing the intersectionality of discrimination, we can work towards creating a more just and equitable society for all.

Chapter 7: Intersectionality and Identity

INTERSECTIONS OF RACE, Gender, and Class

In this book, we will delve into the complex and ever-evolving dynamics that shape the experiences of individuals across these intersecting social categories. By examining the relationships between these three fundamental elements of identity, we aim to shed light on the interconnectedness of social issues, explore the ways in which they intersect and mutually influence one another, and promote a better understanding of diversity, equality, and social justice. Join us on this enlightening journey that aims to unravel the intricacies of race, gender, and class in today's society.

Understanding Intersectionality

To embark on our exploration, we must first grasp the concept of intersectionality. Coined by legal scholar Kimberlé Crenshaw, intersectionality refers to the overlapping and interconnected nature of various social identities, particularly race, gender, and class. It recognizes that individuals experience the world through a multifaceted lens that is shaped by these factors and more. By acknowledging the complex interplay of these dimensions, we can gain a more comprehensive understanding of individuals' experiences and challenges they face within multiple systems of oppression and privilege.

Historical Roots and Contemporary Context

In this one, we will delve into the historical foundations that have shaped the intersections of race, gender, and class throughout different epochs. From the systemic subjugation of marginalized groups to the struggles and triumphs of resistance movements, we will explore how historical events and structures have influenced the present. Additionally, we will examine the current social, political, and economic landscapes to understand their impact on individuals who navigate the complex web of intersecting identities.

Intersections of Race, Gender, and Class in Society

Drawing on sociological research and lived experiences, this one will explore the ways in which race, gender, and class intersect within various social systems. We will uncover the disparities and biases that exist within educational institutions, the workplace, healthcare systems, criminal justice, and other aspects of society. By examining these systems, we aim to promote awareness and foster a dialogue that encourages transformative change.

Beyond Binary Perspectives and Inclusivity

In this one, we will challenge traditional notions of binary thinking and explore more inclusive approaches to understanding and addressing the intersections of race, gender, and class. By considering the experiences of individuals who fall outside the confines of conventional categories, such as non-binary or multiracial individuals, we aim to foster a more inclusive society that embraces diversity in all its forms. Emphasizing the importance of intersectionality in dismantling inequality, we will discuss strategies for promoting inclusivity in both personal and systemic contexts.

Activism, Allyship, and Social Change

Effective allyship requires a deep understanding of the intersections of race, gender, and class. In this one, we will explore ways in which individuals can become allies and advocates for marginalized communities. By examining historical and contemporary examples of activism, we aim to provide practical guidance on how to dismantle oppressive systems and work towards a more equitable society. We will discuss the importance of self-reflection, empathy, and active engagement as crucial steps toward social change.

Intersectionality in the Future

In our final one, we will look toward the future and consider the possibilities for change and progress. By harnessing the knowledge gained throughout this book, we will envision a future that embraces intersectionality as the foundation for social justice. We will explore the role of education, policy, and cultural shifts in creating a more equitable society that empowers individuals irrespective of their race, gender, or class. Through continued dialogue, action, and collective efforts, we can work towards a future that recognizes and celebrates the uniqueness and interconnectedness of all human experiences.

AS WE CONCLUDE THIS journey through the intersections of race, gender, and class, we hope you now have a deeper understanding of the intricacies of these social categories and how they shape individuals' experiences in society. By recognizing the interconnected nature of these identities, we can strive for a society that dismantles systems of oppression and upholds principles of equality and justice. Armed with this knowledge, it is our collective responsibility to create a more inclusive and equitable world for all. Let us work together to navigate the intersections of race, gender, and class and build a brighter future for generations to come.

Navigating Multiple Identities

These identities can be shaped by factors such as race, ethnicity, nationality, gender, sexual orientation, religion, and socio-economic background. Navigating through these various aspects of one's identity can be both challenging and rewarding. This book aims to delve into the intricacies of navigating multiple identities, examining the impact they have on individuals' lives, and offering guidance and insights on how best to manage and embrace these diverse facets of self.

Understanding Multiple Identities

To navigate multiple identities successfully, it is vital to first comprehend the concept of identities themselves. An identity is not a fixed entity but rather a complex web of attributes, beliefs, values, and experiences that shape who we are. It is crucial to acknowledge that identities are not mutually exclusive but rather intersect and overlap, resulting in the formation of unique and multifaceted individuals. By understanding the fluid nature of identities, we can begin to explore the challenges and opportunities presented by navigating multiple identities.

Impact of Multiple Identities on Personal Development

The navigation of multiple identities can significantly impact an individual's personal growth and development. The combination of various identities can provide individuals with diverse perspectives, enabling them to cultivate empathy, adaptability, and open-mindedness. However, these identities can also lead to internal conflicts and external pressures. Successfully navigating multiple identities requires the development of a strong sense of self and the ability to reconcile different aspects of one's identity while embracing and celebrating one's unique background and experiences.

Social and Cultural Contexts of Multiple Identities

The social and cultural contexts within which we exist play a pivotal role in shaping our multiple identities. Social norms, customs, and expectations may influence the way we perceive and prioritize our different identities. It is vital to explore how societal structures and cultural norms impact our ability to navigate and express our multiple identities authentically. By understanding these contexts, we can better comprehend the challenges individuals face in embracing their multiple identities and work towards creating inclusive environments that foster acceptance and understanding.

Challenges and Opportunities of Navigating Multiple Identities

Navigating multiple identities can present individuals with a myriad of challenges and opportunities. The challenges may include managing conflicting expectations, dealing with discrimination or bias, and finding a sense of belonging within different communities. However, these challenges can also offer unique opportunities for growth, self-reflection, and building resilience. By exploring these challenges and opportunities, individuals can develop strategies to overcome obstacles and thrive within their multifaceted identities.

Intersectionality and Multiple Identities

Intersectionality, a concept coined by legal scholar Kimberlé Crenshaw, refers to the interconnected nature of multiple social identities and the unique experiences and challenges that arise from these intersections. Understanding intersectionality is crucial for navigating multiple identities and recognizing that issues and oppressions faced by individuals are often complex and multifaceted. By acknowledging the intersectionality of our identities and fostering inclusivity, we can create a more equitable and just society for all.

Strategies for Navigating Multiple Identities

In this one, we explore various strategies that can help individuals effectively navigate their multiple identities. These strategies may include self-reflection and introspection, seeking support from trusted communities, educating oneself about different cultures and experiences, developing empathy and active listening skills, and embracing a growth mindset. By consciously practicing these strategies, individuals can cultivate a personal toolkit that enables them to navigate multiple identities with confidence and authenticity.

NAVIGATING MULTIPLE identities is a dynamic and ongoing process that requires self-awareness, empathy, and a willingness to embrace diversity. By understanding the complex nature of identities, recognizing the impact of social and cultural contexts, and developing strategies to navigate challenges, individuals can successfully navigate their multifaceted identities while fostering inclusivity and understanding within society. Embracing and celebrating multiple identities can lead to personal growth, enriched relationships, and a more harmonious and interconnected world.

Chapter 8: Cultural Celebrations and Traditions

SIGNIFICANCE OF CULTURAL Festivals

These vibrant celebrations bring communities together to partake in various artistic, culinary, and cultural experiences, fostering a sense of unity and solidarity. In this essay, we will explore the profound significance of cultural festivals, both as a means of preserving cultural heritage and as a catalyst for intercultural understanding and harmony.

Preserving Cultural Heritage:

One of the primary functions of cultural festivals is to preserve and promote a society's cultural heritage. These festivals serve as invaluable platforms for passing down traditional knowledge, customs, and values from one generation to the next. By actively engaging in rituals, art forms, and performances, communities can ensure the survival of their unique cultural identity.

Through various forms of artistic expression, such as music, dance, theater, and storytelling, cultural festivals breathe life into traditions that might otherwise fade away in the face of globalization. Festivals become a powerful medium for oral history, folklore, and traditional craftsmanship, providing both education and entertainment to participants and spectators.

By preserving cultural heritage through festivals, communities develop a collective memory that links the past, present, and future. This continuity fosters a sense of pride and belonging among individuals, strengthening their connection to their roots, and building a cohesive society.

Unifying Communities:

Cultural festivals serve as a dynamic force that unifies communities, irrespective of their socio-economic backgrounds, ethnicity, or religious affiliations. These festivals create opportunities for individuals to come together, breaking down societal barriers and fostering a spirit of inclusivity and understanding.

In celebrating cultural festivals, individuals gain an appreciation for diverse customs, rituals, and ways of life. The act of experiencing and sharing cultural practices helps build bridges of empathy, respect, and tolerance. Festivals bring people from different backgrounds into close proximity, encouraging dialogue, exchange, and the forging of new relationships. Within the festival context, individuals can engage in open-minded discussions, challenging stereotypes, and cultivating mutual respect.

Significantly, the festival experience also encourages cross-cultural communication, enabling the exchange of ideas, artistic expressions, and traditions. Witnessing cultural celebrations outside one's own community broadens perspectives, dispels misconceptions, and enhances intercultural understanding.

Economic Impact and Tourism:

Cultural festivals contribute to the economic growth of local communities, often becoming significant sources of revenue and employment opportunities. These events attract visitors from near and far, stimulating local businesses, such as hotels, restaurants, and artisans. A well-organized cultural festival can revitalize a community, creating a thriving market for local products, crafts, and services.

Furthermore, cultural festivals play a vital role in the promotion of tourism. They act as powerful magnets, attracting visitors curious to explore the distinctive heritage and customs of different regions. Travelers seeking authentic cultural experiences are drawn to festivals, resulting in increased tourist numbers and boosting the local economy.

In addition to economic benefits, cultural festivals can also enhance a region's international reputation. By showcasing the unique aspects of local culture, festivals create positive visibility that helps shape a region's image. This positive branding attracts investment, encourages cultural exchange, and promotes cultural diplomacy, leading to enhanced global understanding and cooperation.

CULTURAL FESTIVALS are much more than mere celebrations; they are profound expressions and preservers of cultural heritage. These events unite communities, fostering inclusivity and understanding, while also contributing to economic growth and promoting tourism. By actively participating in celebrations of cultural festivals, individuals not only embrace their own cultural roots but also cultivate appreciation and respect for the diversity that enriches our global society. Cultural festivals, with their power to connect people and bridge differences, are essential in fostering a world of harmony and recognition of our shared humanity.

Importance of Preserving Cultural Heritage

One key reason why preserving cultural heritage is crucial is the role it plays in fostering a sense of identity and belonging among individuals. Cultural heritage connects individuals to their roots, providing them with a unique sense of self and a deeper understanding of their place in the world. It helps people recognize the contributions of their ancestors and the struggles they went through, instilling a sense of pride in one's cultural heritage. This knowledge of our past can empower individuals and communities, leading to greater self-confidence and a stronger sense of cohesion within the society.

Furthermore, cultural heritage acts as a bridge between generations, allowing us to trace our lineage and comprehend the historical context in which our ancestors lived. By preserving our cultural heritage, we are ensuring that future generations will have access to the stories, traditions, and practices that have shaped their collective identity. Children growing up with a connection to their cultural heritage are more likely to embrace diversity, value their own heritage, and respect other cultures. This understanding and appreciation of cultural differences can contribute to building more inclusive and tolerant societies, fostering peace and understanding in an increasingly globalized world.

Another aspect of cultural heritage that makes its preservation vital is the opportunity it provides for economic growth and sustainable development. Cultural tourism has become an important industry, attracting visitors from all over the world to explore cultural landmarks, cultural festivals, and historical sites. Preservation and promotion of cultural heritage therefore not only help to generate revenue for communities but also support job creation and entrepreneurship. Local artisans, craftsmen, and cultural experts benefit from the interest and demand for traditional arts, craftwork, and cultural experiences. Thus, cultural preservation serves as a powerful tool for generating income and promoting sustainable development, particularly in regions with rich cultural heritage.

Preserving cultural heritage also contributes to the field of education and research. Cultural artifacts, ancient manuscripts, and historical documents provide invaluable insights into the past, enabling scholars and researchers to study and interpret the various aspects of a bygone era. By preserving these artifacts, we are preserving a tangible link to history, allowing future researchers to access primary sources and draw s based on first-hand evidence. This exchange of knowledge through research and education helps us uncover new dimensions of our shared history and enables us to learn from the mistakes and successes of those who came before us.

Furthermore, cultural heritage preservation has a profound impact on our well-being and overall quality of life. Cultural traditions and practices often bring communities together, providing an avenue for social interaction and cohesion. Participating in cultural activities and festivals fosters a sense of belonging and enhances social capital. It helps to build strong and supportive communities where individuals can connect with one another, share experiences, and learn from different perspectives.

In addition to the social benefits, cultural heritage preservation also contributes to the aesthetic beauty of a community. Traditional architecture, historic sites, and cultural landmarks add character and charm to neighborhoods, making them distinct and visually appealing. Preserving these elements not only enriches the local environment but also attracts tourists and boosts the community's economy.

While the importance of preserving cultural heritage is evident, it is unfortunate that cultural artifacts and heritage sites are often vulnerable to various threats. Urbanization, natural disasters, armed conflicts, globalization, neglect, and even climate change pose significant risks to our cultural heritage. Therefore, it is imperative for governments, organizations, and individuals to prioritize the preservation and protection of cultural heritage through sustainable policies, robust legislation, and international cooperation. Cultural heritage serves as a source of identity, a link between generations, a catalyst for economic growth, a medium for education and research, a driver of social well-being, and a reflection of our aesthetic and historical values. By safeguarding and promoting cultural heritage, we can preserve the diverse tapestry of human civilization and contribute to a more inclusive, informed, and prosperous world.

Chapter 9: Education and Empowerment

ROLE OF EDUCATION IN Empowering Communities

One of the most significant ways in which education empowers communities is through the development of critical thinking and problem-solving skills. By engaging in formal education systems, individuals are encouraged to think independently, analyze information, and form their own opinions. This ability to think critically and creatively is crucial in empowering communities, as it allows individuals to identify and address societal issues and challenges. Education fosters a culture of proactive problem-solving, empowering individuals to seek innovative solutions to both individual and community problems. Furthermore, education cultivates a sense of ownership and responsibility towards one's community, motivating individuals to actively contribute to its development and well-being.

Education also plays a crucial role in empowering communities by promoting social cohesion and inclusivity. In many societies, education is a means of breaking down social barriers and promoting equal opportunities for all members. By providing individuals from diverse backgrounds equal access to education, communities can combat discrimination and promote social justice. Education acts as a social equalizer, enabling individuals from marginalized communities to overcome systemic barriers and create a more inclusive society. Moreover, education has the power to challenge stereotypes and promote cultural understanding, fostering a sense of belonging and cohesion within communities. This inclusive approach to education empowers communities by ensuring that each member has an equal chance to thrive and contribute to society.

Furthermore, education serves as a pathway to economic empowerment for individuals and communities. A well-rounded education equips individuals with the skills and knowledge needed to enter and succeed in the job market.

By acquiring relevant qualifications and skills, individuals can secure employment that ensures a sustainable livelihood, lifting themselves and their communities out of poverty. Additionally, education instills a sense of entrepreneurship and innovation, enabling individuals to create their own opportunities and contribute to the local economy. When individuals within a community are economically empowered, it leads to increased prosperity and improved living conditions, benefiting not only themselves but also the wider community.

Education is not limited to traditional formal schooling; it extends beyond classroom walls and encompasses lifelong learning opportunities. Lifelong learning empowers individuals to continually update their skills, adapt to evolving circumstances, and stay relevant in an ever-changing world. By embracing lifelong learning, individuals can remain competitive in the job market, leading to increased economic empowerment and improved community development. Moreover, lifelong learning fosters personal growth and self-fulfillment, enabling individuals to discover their passions and pursue their dreams. This self-empowerment translates into community empowerment, as individuals contribute their unique talents and strengths towards the betterment of their communities.

In order to maximize the role of education in empowering communities, there are several key considerations that need to be addressed. Firstly, the accessibility and quality of education must be ensured for all members of society, regardless of their socio-economic background or geographical location. This requires investment in educational infrastructure, including schools, educational materials, and qualified teachers. Moreover, it necessitates the implementation of inclusive educational policies that embrace diversity and promote equal opportunities. By addressing these fundamental issues, communities can ensure that education is a truly empowering force that reaches everyone.

Secondly, education must be tailored to the specific needs and aspirations of communities. This involves incorporating local knowledge, culture, and values into the curriculum, making education more relevant and meaningful for learners. By embracing community-specific content and utilizing local resources, education can foster a sense of belonging and identity within communities. Additionally, education should equip individuals with the practical skills needed for sustainable community development, such as environmental stewardship, entrepreneurship, and leadership. By aligning education with community needs, it becomes a powerful tool for transformation and empowerment.

Lastly, partnerships and collaboration between various stakeholders are essential in empowering communities through education. Governments, non-governmental organizations, community leaders, and educators must work together to formulate and implement effective educational policies and strategies. This collaborative approach ensures that educational resources are utilized optimally and that the diverse needs of communities are met. By fostering strong partnerships, communities can create a supportive educational ecosystem that empowers individuals and leads to sustainable community development. Education equips individuals with the necessary skills, knowledge, and mindset to actively participate in society and contribute to the well-being of their communities. It promotes critical thinking, social cohesion, economic empowerment, and lifelong learning. To fully harness the power of education as an empowering force, accessibility, quality, relevance, and collaboration are essential. By addressing these factors, communities can leverage education to build a more inclusive, equitable, and prosperous future.

Chapter 10: Media Representation

IMPACT OF MEDIA ON Perceptions of Race

One of the primary ways that media influences perceptions of race is through the portrayal of racial stereotypes. Stereotypes are oversimplified generalizations about a particular racial group, often based on limited information or biased perspectives. Media, particularly popular culture, has a long history of perpetuating and reinforcing racial stereotypes. For example, African Americans have frequently been depicted as criminals or athletes, Asian Americans as nerdy or exotic, and Latinos as gang members or gardeners. These representations can shape public perception and reinforce biases, leading to unfair treatment and discrimination in real-life situations.

Moreover, media can contribute to the creation and reinforcement of racial hierarchies. By consistently presenting certain racial groups in positions of power and authority, while marginalizing or stereotyping others, media can perpetuate the idea that some races are superior or inferior to others. This can have profound implications for how individuals perceive their own racial identity and how they interact with people from different racial backgrounds. For example, media that consistently portrays white individuals as successful leaders while depicting people of color as sidekicks or villains may lead to the internalization of racial hierarchies and the reinforcement of white privilege.

The impact of media on perceptions of race is also influenced by the lack of diversity in media representation. Historically, and still to a large extent today, media industries have been predominantly controlled by white individuals, resulting in a limited range of perspectives and experiences being represented. This lack of diversity can lead to inaccurate and incomplete portrayals of racial groups, reinforcing existing stereotypes and biases. Furthermore, the underrepresentation of people of color in media can contribute to feelings of exclusion and marginalization, reinforcing racial inequalities and limiting opportunities for minority groups.

However, it is important to note that media can also play a positive role in shaping perceptions of race. When media platforms feature diverse and inclusive representations of different racial groups, it can challenge stereotypes and promote a more nuanced understanding of race. For example, the increased visibility of strong and complex Black characters in recent years has been celebrated as a step towards dismantling racial stereotypes and promoting more diverse narratives. Likewise, media that focuses on the experiences and perspectives of people of color can help to counteract the dominant white-centric narratives that have historically dominated media.

To address the impact of media on perceptions of race, it is crucial to promote media literacy and critical thinking skills among consumers. Teaching individuals how to critically analyze media messages, identify stereotypes, and challenge biased representations can empower them to resist the negative effects of media on perceptions of race. Furthermore, initiatives aimed at increasing diversity and representation in media production and decision-making positions can help to promote more accurate and inclusive portrayals of racial groups. Media can shape our attitudes, beliefs, and prejudices about different racial groups by perpetuating stereotypes, contributing to racial hierarchies, and reinforcing biases. However, media also has the potential to challenge stereotypes and promote a more inclusive understanding of race when diverse and accurate representations are prioritized. By promoting media literacy and enhancing diversity in media representation, we can work towards a more equitable and inclusive society, where race is understood and celebrated in all its complexities.

Promoting Diversity in Media

Diversity in media refers to the fair and equal representation of various racial, ethnic, gender, sexual orientation, socio-economic, and cultural groups in all forms of media, including television, film, journalism, advertising, and digital platforms. It goes beyond the mere inclusion of diverse characters or token representation but encompasses the need for authentic and nuanced portrayals that break stereotypes and challenge societal biases.

One of the key reasons to promote diversity in media is the power it has to shape public opinion and cultural understanding. When we see individuals from different backgrounds and identities in media, it helps to dispel stereotypes and reinforces the idea that diversity is not only accepted but celebrated. This, in turn, can foster empathy, tolerance, and a greater understanding of our shared humanity. By providing a platform for underrepresented voices to be heard, media can help bridge gaps of understanding and create a more inclusive society.

Furthermore, promoting diversity in media is essential for providing role models and inspiring future generations. When marginalized communities see themselves represented in media, it not only boosts their self-esteem but also opens up a world of possibilities. By showcasing diverse voices and stories, media can encourage individuals from all backgrounds to pursue their dreams, while also breaking down barriers that hinder progress and achievement.

In addition to these social and cultural benefits, diversity in media also makes good business sense. The global marketplace is becoming increasingly diverse, and companies that fail to reflect this diversity in their advertising and marketing efforts risk alienating potential customers. By promoting diversity in media, companies can tap into a broader consumer base and reach new audiences. Moreover, studies have consistently shown that diverse teams, whether in media production or content creation, result in better decision-making, creativity, and innovation. Therefore, it is not only a moral imperative but also a strategic advantage for companies to ensure diversity in their media representation.

While the importance of promoting diversity in media is clear, the question of how to achieve it remains. There are several key strategies that can be employed to increase diversity in media.

Firstly, media organizations and content creators must make a conscious effort to actively seek out and amplify voices from marginalized communities. This can be done through targeted outreach, fostering relationships with diverse talent, and creating inclusive spaces that welcome diverse perspectives. By providing opportunities and platforms for underrepresented individuals, media organizations can help overcome the systematic barriers that often exclude certain groups from participation.

Secondly, media organizations should also examine their own internal practices and culture. Diverse representation should not only be limited to on-screen or byline presence but should permeate throughout all levels of the industry. This means diversifying hiring practices, creating mentorship and career development programs for underrepresented groups, and fostering an inclusive work environment where all employees feel valued and respected.

Thirdly, educational institutions have a crucial role to play in promoting diversity in media. By offering diverse and inclusive curricula, media programs can help train the next generation of content creators and journalists to recognize and challenge biases and stereotypes. Additionally, collaboration between educational institutions and media organizations can provide opportunities for aspiring media professionals from marginalized backgrounds to gain experience and expertise.

Lastly, consumers can also play an active role in promoting diversity in media. By supporting and consuming content created by diverse voices, audiences can send a clear message to media organizations that representation matters. Engaging in open dialogue, both online and offline, and holding media organizations accountable for their actions or lack thereof can also drive change. By accurately representing the diverse range of people and experiences in our society, media can shape public opinion, foster understanding, and inspire future generations. To achieve diversity in media, it requires collective action from media organizations, content creators, educational institutions, and consumers. By embracing diversity, we can create a media landscape that reflects the world we live in and strive for a society that celebrates and values the richness of its differences.

Chapter 11: Labor and Economic Justice

CHALLENGES FACED BY Minority Workers

However, minority workers continue to face unique challenges that hinder their professional growth and well-being. This one aims to shed light on these obstacles and offer insights into addressing them effectively. By understanding and addressing these challenges head-on, organizations can create an environment where all employees, regardless of their background, can thrive and contribute to the fullest. Let us explore the key challenges faced by minority workers and delve into strategies to promote a more inclusive workplace.

1. Bias and Prejudice in Hiring Practices:

One of the primary hurdles faced by minority workers is bias and prejudice in the hiring process. Historical inequalities and societal stereotypes often seep into recruitment, leading to unconscious biases and favoritism towards certain groups. To address this challenge, organizations must adopt proactive measures such as blind screening processes and diversifying recruitment panels. By eliminating identifiable information from resumes and ensuring a diverse set of evaluators, employers can mitigate biases and promote fair and equal hiring practices.

2. Limited Access to Opportunities:

Minority workers often find themselves limited by systemic barriers that restrict their access to career advancement opportunities. This may manifest as limited access to mentorship programs, leadership roles, or high-visibility projects. To address this challenge, organizations can implement mentorship initiatives specifically designed to support minority employees, creating a network of guidance and support. Furthermore, transparent career development frameworks and targeted training programs can empower underrepresented individuals, enabling them to acquire the necessary skills and qualifications to advance their careers.

3. Workplace Discrimination and Harassment:

A distressing reality for many minority workers is the presence of discrimination and harassment in the workplace. Experiencing discrimination based on race, ethnicity, gender, or other protected characteristics can significantly impact an individual's well-being and career progression. Addressing discrimination requires the integration of robust policies against harassment and bias, coupled with training programs designed to educate employees on respectful conduct and bystander intervention. Creating a culture of zero-tolerance towards discrimination empowers minority workers to feel safe, supported, and valued.

4. Lack of Representation and Voice:

A significant challenge faced by minority workers is the lack of representation and the absence of their voices in decision-making processes. This can perpetuate feelings of exclusion and marginalization. Organizations must actively seek to diversify leadership positions and boardrooms, ensuring that minority voices are respected and included in discussions that shape the company's direction. Employee resource groups and affinity networks can also provide safe spaces for minority employees to voice their concerns and collaborate on initiatives that promote diversity and inclusion.

5. Microaggressions and Stereotyping:

Microaggressions, subtle acts of discrimination or hostility, are a pervasive challenge faced by minority workers. These can include offensive comments, insensitive questions, or exclusionary behavior. Organizations must prioritize education and training to help employees recognize and address microaggressions. Building empathy and cultural intelligence through diversity training programs fosters a respectful and inclusive work environment, reducing the impact of stereotypes and microaggressions on minority workers.

THE CHALLENGES FACED by minority workers are complex and multifaceted, requiring a concerted effort from organizations to address them effectively. By acknowledging and actively working towards eliminating bias in hiring practices, increasing access to opportunities for career advancement, combatting discrimination and harassment, promoting representation and inclusion, and addressing microaggressions, organizations can create a workplace that celebrates diversity and empowers all employees. By fostering a culture of equity and inclusivity, organizations not only benefit individual employees but also build stronger teams, enhance innovation, and drive better business outcomes. Let us strive to make our workplaces truly inclusive, valuing the contributions and experiences of every individual, regardless of their background.

Strategies for Economic Empowerment

It refers to the process of enabling individuals and communities to have control over their financial resources, access to economic opportunities, and the ability to participate fully in economic decision-making. To ensure sustainable economic empowerment, it is essential to employ effective strategies that address multiple dimensions of inequality, including gender, race, ethnicity, and socio-economic status. In this one, we will explore various strategies for economic empowerment and their significance in promoting inclusive growth, reducing poverty, and fostering social development.

1. Enhancing Education and Skills Development:

Education and skills development are crucial drivers of economic empowerment. To effectively participate in the labor market and entrepreneurial activities, individuals need access to quality education that equips them with relevant skills and knowledge. Governments and organizations should focus on strengthening the education system, providing equal educational opportunities for all, and offering vocational training programs that align with the needs of the job market. Additionally, investing in continuous skills development and providing lifelong learning opportunities is vital to ensure individuals remain competitive and adaptable in a rapidly changing economy.

2. Promoting Financial Inclusion:

Access to financial services, particularly for marginalized communities, is a key enabler of economic empowerment. Financial inclusion involves providing individuals and small businesses with affordable and convenient access to formal financial services such as savings accounts, credit, insurance, and payment systems. This can be achieved through the establishment of community-based banks, mobile banking services, and microfinance institutions. Additionally, financial literacy programs should be implemented to educate individuals on money management, budgeting, and savings, enabling them to make informed financial decisions and build assets.

3. Fostering Entrepreneurship and Small Business Development:

Entrepreneurship plays a crucial role in creating job opportunities, promoting innovation, and driving economic growth. To empower individuals to start and sustain their own businesses, governments and organizations should provide comprehensive support systems. This includes access to capital through loans and grants, business development services such as mentorship and training, and the creation of an enabling environment that removes regulatory barriers and promotes a culture of entrepreneurship. By fostering small business development, economic empowerment can be extended to a broader section of society, particularly those who face discrimination in traditional employment settings.

4. Advancing Gender Equality in the Workplace:

Achieving gender equality is not only a matter of social justice but also a prerequisite for sustainable economic development. Gender disparities in the workplace, such as unequal pay and limited access to leadership positions, hinder women's economic empowerment. To address these challenges, policies and initiatives should be implemented to promote gender-equal hiring practices, provide equal pay for equal work, and create a supportive work environment that enables work-life balance. Increasing the representation of women in managerial and decision-making roles is also crucial to ensure their voices are heard and their perspectives are taken into account.

5. Strengthening Social Safety Nets:

Social safety nets play a crucial role in preventing individuals and communities from falling into poverty and help buffer the impact of economic shocks. Strengthening these safety nets is essential to ensure that vulnerable populations have access to basic needs such as healthcare, education, and food security. Governments should invest in comprehensive social protection programs that provide income support, unemployment benefits, healthcare, and retirement savings options. By providing a safety net, individuals can take more risks, invest in education or entrepreneurship, and ultimately achieve economic empowerment.

6. Encouraging Sustainable Development:

Economic empowerment cannot be achieved at the expense of the environment or future generations. Sustainable development focuses on meeting the needs of the present without compromising the ability of future generations to meet their own needs. Governments and organizations should adopt sustainable development strategies that promote responsible consumption and production, invest in clean energy, and implement environmentally friendly practices. By prioritizing sustainability, economic empowerment can be achieved in a manner that preserves natural resources and fosters long-term economic resilience.

STRATEGIES FOR ECONOMIC empowerment encompass a range of interventions that promote equal access to education, financial services, employment opportunities, and entrepreneurial support. By implementing these strategies, individuals and communities can break free from the cycle of poverty, achieve self-reliance, and contribute to overall social development. It is imperative that governments, organizations, and individuals work together to enact and sustain these strategies, ensuring that economic empowerment becomes a universal reality. Only through such collaborative efforts can we move closer to a world where everyone has the opportunity to fulfill their economic potential and enjoy a life of dignity and prosperity.

Chapter 12: Community Organizations and Activism

GRASSROOTS EFFORTS for Social Change

This book explores the multifaceted nature of grassroots movements, shedding light on their origins, significance, and impact on various social issues. With a focus on empowering communities and fostering positive change, this comprehensive analysis aims to provide insight into the methods, strategies, and emerging trends associated with grassroots efforts. By delving into this topic, readers will gain a deeper understanding of the potential for bottom-up initiatives to reshape society and contribute to lasting change.

Understanding Grassroots Movements

1.1 Defining Grassroots Efforts

Grassroots efforts encompass a variety of initiatives driven by individuals, local groups, or communities, aimed at addressing social, political, or environmental issues. Unlike mainstream movements, grassroots initiatives often arise organically from the needs and concerns of ordinary people, rather than being led by established organizations or influential figures. This one will explore the fundamental characteristics that distinguish grassroots efforts, emphasizing their bottom-up nature, inclusivity, and commitment to community engagement.

1.2 Historical Roots of Grassroots Movements

Grassroots movements have a rich history deeply embedded in social activism and political reform. From the civil rights movement in the United States to the anti-apartheid struggle in South Africa, numerous historical examples illustrate the power of grassroots mobilization in effecting change. By examining past movements' successes, failures, and strategies, this one will provide valuable insight into the lessons learned and the broader context underpinning contemporary grassroots efforts.

Facilitating Grassroots Activism

2.1 Mobilizing Communities

At the core of any effective grassroots effort lies the ability to mobilize communities towards a common goal. This one will explore the strategies and methods used to engage individuals and promote active participation. Techniques such as community organizing, public awareness campaigns, and building alliances will be discussed, providing readers with practical guidance on igniting social change at the grassroots level.

2.2 Technology and Grassroots Advocacy

The digital age has revolutionized the methods through which grassroots movements operate. This one will illustrate the powerful role that technology and social media play in fostering connectivity and amplifying voices. From crowdfunding platforms to online petitions, these technological advancements have greatly enhanced the reach and impact of grassroots activism.

Grassroots Efforts and Socioeconomic Change

3.1 Addressing Economic Inequality

Grassroots movements frequently emerge as responses to deep-rooted economic inequalities. This one will delve into the ways in which grassroots efforts strive to combat poverty, inequality, and social exclusion. By fostering economic empowerment, mobilizing marginalized groups, and advocating for fair labor practices, grassroots initiatives have the potential to uplift communities and create sustainable change.

3.2 Environmental Justice at the Grassroots Level

Recognizing the interconnectedness between social and environmental issues, grassroots movements have increasingly focused on promoting environmental justice. This one will explore the initiatives aimed at combating climate change, protecting ecosystems, and advocating for sustainable practices within local communities. By empowering individuals to take action at the grassroots level, these efforts serve as a catalyst for broader environmental change.

Grassroots Movements and Policy Change

4.1 Influence on Local Policies

Grassroots movements possess the power to influence local policies by bridging gaps between communities and policymakers. This one will examine successful campaigns that have resulted in meaningful legislative changes at the local level. It will also explore strategies for effective advocacy, such as community organizing, coalition building, and engaging with policymakers, to inspire readers to take action and effect policy change within their own communities.

4.2 Lessons from Grassroots Initiatives

Drawing upon case studies and real-life examples, this one will distill valuable lessons from grassroots movements worldwide. By highlighting successful strategies, ethical considerations, and potential challenges, readers will gain a broader understanding of the key elements necessary for grassroots activism to thrive and drive sustainable social change.

GRASSROOTS EFFORTS for social change represent a vital pathway towards a more just and equitable society. By understanding the principles, strategies, and impact of grassroots movements, individuals can harness the collective power of communities to address pressing social, political, and environmental challenges. This book aims to inspire readers to actively engage in grassroots initiatives, fostering a culture of empowerment, inclusivity, and activism in pursuit of a better future for all. Through the lens of grassroots efforts, we can collectively shape a more socially conscious and compassionate world.

Building Stronger Communities through Activism

Activism, a powerful tool for social change, plays a vital role in creating and sustaining these stronger communities. By harnessing the collective voice and action of individuals, activism has the potential to address systemic injustices, promote solidarity, and bring about lasting positive transformations. In this book, we delve into the importance of activism in building stronger communities, exploring its various forms, strategies, and the remarkable impact it can have on society.

Understanding Activism and Community Strength

To embark on our exploration, it is essential first to establish a common understanding of what activism entails and how it contributes to building stronger communities. Activism refers to the deliberate efforts taken to challenge unjust systems, promote social change, and advocate for the rights and well-being of individuals and communities. It involves various forms, including grassroots movements, advocacy campaigns, protests, and community organizing. By actively engaging in actions that challenge the status quo, activists aim to empower individuals, address inequalities, and foster a sense of belonging and unity within their communities.

The Role of Activism in Fostering Inclusivity and Representation

One of the fundamental pillars of building stronger communities is ensuring inclusivity and representation for all individuals, regardless of their background. Activism acts as a catalyst in this regard, raising awareness about marginalized groups, amplifying their voices, and advocating for their inclusion at every level of society. Through initiatives such as affirmative action, policy reforms, and awareness campaigns, activists strive to dismantle discriminatory structures and promote social equity. By fostering inclusivity and representation, communities become more resilient, diverse, and cohesive, ensuring that no one feels left behind or unheard.

Activism as a Means to Address Social Injustices

A key driving force behind activism is the need to combat and address social injustices that persist in our society. Communities plagued by inequality, discrimination, or oppression rely on activists to shed light on these issues and work towards dismantling such unjust systems. Activists challenge biases and prejudices, advocating for equal rights, fair treatment, and access to resources for all individuals. By recognizing and addressing these injustices head-on, communities can become stronger, more empathetic, and equitable, fostering an environment where everyone can thrive.

The Power of Collective Action in Community-Building

The beauty of activism lies in its ability to mobilize individuals towards a common goal, igniting a sense of unity and collective purpose within communities. By organizing grassroots movements, conducting protests, and establishing community-led initiatives, activists showcase the power of collective action in shaping societal norms and attitudes. The shared experiences, struggles, and triumphs that arise from such efforts contribute to a stronger community fabric, fostering connections and promoting collaboration among community members. Through collective action, communities can realize their potential for change and resilience.

Activism's Role in Empowering Individuals and Building Capacity

Activism not only addresses societal issues but also creates an empowering environment for individuals within communities. By engaging in activism, individuals gain a sense of agency, recognizing their capacity to effect change and make a difference. Through participation in community-led initiatives, leadership development programs, and skill-building workshops, activists empower individuals to take charge of their own lives, inspiring them to become agents of change in their communities. In turn, this empowerment contributes to the overall strength and sustainability of the community by fostering a culture of self-determination and empowerment.

Sustaining Activism for Long-Term Community Impact

To ensure that activism can create meaningful and lasting impacts, it is crucial to address the challenges and strategies for sustaining these efforts in the long run. Activists must learn how to overcome burnout, maintain momentum, and create avenues for continued engagement. Building partnerships, leveraging technology, and establishing mentorship programs are all strategies that can help sustain activism efforts and maximize their impact on communities. By considering long-term sustainability, activists can ensure that their work continues to build stronger communities for generations to come.

BUILDING STRONGER COMMUNITIES through activism represents a path towards a more just and equitable future. By engaging in collective action, addressing social injustices, and empowering individuals, activists play a vital role in shaping vibrant, resilient, and inclusive communities. As this book has explored, activism is essential for fostering community strength, unity, and social change. It is through the dedication and commitment of activists that we can build a world where every individual feels heard, valued, and supported.

Chapter 13: Healing and Reconciliation

HEALING HISTORICAL Trauma

The wounds of these deeply traumatic events have reverberated through generations, impacting individuals, families, communities, and entire nations. Healing historical trauma is an intricate process that requires acknowledging and understanding historical injustices, promoting restorative justice, and fostering a collective healing journey. In this book, we will explore the nature of historical trauma, its manifestation in different societies, and the strategies for healing, resilience, and reconciliation.

Understanding Historical Trauma

To embark on the path of healing historical trauma, it is crucial to first grasp the nature and impact of intergenerational trauma. Historical trauma refers to the cumulative emotional and psychological harm experienced by individuals and communities as a result of historical events that deeply violated their sense of identity, culture, and sense of safety. This trauma can be transmitted across generations, perpetuating cycles of pain and suffering. By understanding the complex web of historical traumas, we can begin to explore the ways in which it has manifested in different societies around the world.

The Manifestation of Historical Trauma

Through comprehensive research and examination of case studies, this one will delve into the diverse ways in which historical trauma has manifested across cultures and continents. We will explore the historical traumas experienced by Indigenous communities, African descendants, post-colonial nations, and communities affected by war and genocide. By shedding light on these different experiences, we aim to create empathy, understanding, and a platform for collective healing.

Unearthing Historical Trauma

Healing historical trauma necessitates unearthing the often-buried and overlooked stories of trauma and injustice. This one will delve into the importance of truth-telling, the process of acknowledging and validating the experiences of victims, and the ways in which historical narratives shape our understanding of the present. By listening to and centering the voices of those most affected, we can begin to dismantle historical trauma's hold on society.

Restorative Justice and Healing

Restorative justice is an essential component of healing historical trauma. In this one, we will explore various approaches to restorative justice, including truth commissions, reparations, and other mechanisms for reckoning with the past. By highlighting successful examples from around the world, we will demonstrate how restorative justice can contribute to the healing process, fostering reconciliation, and rebuilding fractured communities.

Honoring Resilience and Promoting Well-being

Resilience is a central aspect of healing historical trauma. In this one, we will delve into the remarkable stories of individuals, families, and communities that have faced adversity head-on and still emerged with strength and hope. Additionally, we will explore the importance of promoting holistic well-being, including physical, mental, emotional, and spiritual health. By sharing empowering narratives and discussing evidence-based practices, readers will find inspiration and practical strategies for fostering resilience in their own communities.

The Role of Education in Healing Trauma

Education is a powerful tool for addressing historical trauma. This one will examine the ways in which formal and informal education can contribute to healing, understanding, and empathy. By incorporating honest and inclusive historical narratives, promoting cultural appreciation, and fostering critical thinking, educational institutions can play a crucial role in building a more inclusive and equitable society.

Collective Healing and Reconciliation

The final one focuses on the importance of collective healing and reconciliation as a path towards a more harmonious world. We will explore the significance of dialogue, forgiveness, and accountability in bridging divides and promoting healing. Furthermore, we will highlight successful examples of communities and nations that have embarked on transformative journeys of collective healing, generating lasting change and fostering unity.

HEALING HISTORICAL trauma is a complex and multifaceted process that necessitates a deep understanding of the past, a commitment to truth-telling, and a willingness to engage in restorative justice. By exploring the manifestation of historical trauma in different societies, honoring resilience, promoting well-being, and embracing education's transformative potential, we can take steps towards healing collective wounds and building more inclusive and empathetic communities. The road to healing is not easy, but it is through acknowledging and addressing our shared past that we can pave the way for a brighter and more equitable future.

Promoting Reconciliation Among Different Groups

One of the primary reasons why promoting reconciliation is crucial is the existence of deep-rooted conflicts and divisions between different groups. Whether these divisions are based on ethnicity, religion, nationality, or social status, they can have devastating consequences. They lead to systemic discrimination, prejudice, and violence, perpetuating a cycle of animosity and hostility. Reconciliation aims to break this cycle by fostering understanding, empathy, and respect among different groups. By promoting reconciliation, we can actively work towards healing the wounds of the past and building a shared future based on inclusivity and equality.

However, promoting reconciliation is not an easy task; it poses several challenges. One of the main challenges is the existence of deeply entrenched prejudices and stereotypes. These biases often prevent individuals from fully understanding and empathizing with members of different groups.

Overcoming these biases requires a conscious effort to challenge our own assumptions and engage in meaningful dialogue with others. It necessitates creating spaces that allow for open and honest conversations where individuals can share their experiences, fears, and aspirations. By doing so, we can chip away at the walls that separate us and foster a genuine understanding of the experiences and perspectives of others.

Another significant challenge to promoting reconciliation is the existence of historical injustices. Many conflicts and divisions are rooted in long-standing grievances that have not been adequately addressed. Reconciliation requires acknowledging and addressing these historical injustices, as they serve as significant barriers to healing and progress. This acknowledgment entails a willingness to confront uncomfortable truths about our collective past – acknowledging wrongs committed, taking responsibility for them, and seeking redress. By acknowledging and addressing historical injustices, we can lay the groundwork for genuine reconciliation and create a more equitable society.

Strategies for promoting reconciliation encompass both individual and collective actions. On an individual level, fostering empathy is crucial. Empathy enables us to put ourselves in the shoes of others, to understand their experiences, and to genuinely connect with them. By actively seeking to understand others and their lived realities, we can break down barriers, dismantle stereotypes, and build bridges of understanding. Developing this empathetic mindset requires openness, active listening, and a genuine curiosity about the experiences and perspectives of others.

Another key strategy is promoting dialogue and creating safe spaces for conversations. Dialogue allows individuals from different backgrounds to come together, share their stories, and engage in constructive discussions. It is essential to create an atmosphere of respect and non-judgment where individuals feel safe expressing their opinions and experiences. Meaningful dialogue opens up avenues for shared understanding and can foster the development of mutual trust and respect. By valuing dialogue as a tool for reconciliation, we can create the necessary conditions for bridge-building across diverse groups.

Additionally, promoting reconciliation requires addressing structural and systemic inequities that perpetuate divisions between groups. This involves advocating for policies that promote equality, inclusivity, and social justice. It requires dismantling discriminatory practices, eradicating systemic barriers, and ensuring equal access to opportunities and resources for all members of society. By addressing these structural inequities, we can remove the underlying factors that perpetuate conflicts and divisions and create a more just and reconciled society. It requires us to challenge our biases, acknowledge historical injustices, and actively engage in dialogue and empathy-building. By promoting reconciliation, we can break the cycle of animosity and hostility that divides us and work towards creating a more inclusive and peaceful society. Let this book serve as a guide to understanding the importance of reconciliation, the challenges it poses, and the strategies that can contribute to fostering meaningful connections among diverse groups. Together, we can build a future where reconciliation and understanding prevail.

Chapter 14: Global Perspectives on Race and Culture

INTERNATIONAL EFFORTS for Racial Justice

Addressing issues of racial inequality and discrimination on a global scale requires a collaborative approach that transcends national boundaries. This one aims to shed light on the importance of international efforts for racial justice, exploring key initiatives, organizations, and challenges that lie ahead. By analyzing the multifaceted dynamics of racial justice in a global context, we can cultivate a better understanding of what it takes to bridge societal divides and foster a more inclusive world.

I. Historical Context and Global Challenges:

To fully comprehend the dynamics of international efforts for racial justice, acknowledging the historical context is crucial. Racial injustice can be traced back to the colonial era, when notions of racial superiority and inferiority were perpetuated to serve the interests of ruling classes. The legacy of colonization has left deep-rooted inequalities and prejudices that persist to this day.

One of the most significant global challenges is dismantling systemic racism. This requires recognizing that racial discrimination exists in various forms such as institutional racism, structural violence, and implicit biases. Overcoming these challenges necessitates a comprehensive approach that includes legal reforms, education, and economic empowerment.

II. The Role of International Organizations:

Numerous international organizations have played pivotal roles in advancing racial justice. The United Nations (UN) and its subsidiary bodies, such as the Committee on the Elimination of Racial Discrimination (CERD), have been at the forefront of these efforts. CERD monitors states' compliance with the International Convention on the Elimination of All Forms of Racial Discrimination. Such mechanisms empower countries and civil society organizations to work collectively towards eradicating racial discrimination and promoting social justice.

Furthermore, regional organizations like the African Union (AU), the European Union (EU), and the Organization of American States (OAS) have been instrumental in fostering dialogue and cooperation among member states. These platforms facilitate the exchange of best practices, promote policy harmonization, and advocate for the establishment of inclusive legal frameworks.

III. Grassroots Movements and Civil Society Activism:

While international organizations play a significant role, grassroots movements and civil society activism have proven to be catalysts for change in the pursuit of racial justice. Movements like Black Lives Matter (BLM) have captured the attention of the global community, sparking conversations and awareness about systemic racism. Such movements have mobilized activists, academics, and artists alike, inspiring a collective quest for equality.

Community-based organizations have also emerged as linchpins in the fight against racial injustice. These organizations provide crucial support, resources, and education to affected communities, contributing to the empowerment of marginalized individuals and their communities. Their efforts often include initiatives aimed at bridging racial divides, promoting dialogue, and fostering understanding.

IV. Education and Cultural Exchange:

Education and cultural exchange programs have proven to be transformative tools for promoting racial justice. By fostering cross-cultural understanding and empathy, these initiatives can challenge stereotypes, prejudices, and biases. Furthermore, educational curricula that accurately reflect diverse histories and narratives can help debunk racial stereotypes, enhance critical thinking, and encourage inclusivity.

International exchange programs, like the Fulbright Program, offer scholars and students opportunities to study and collaborate across borders, fostering global perspectives on racial justice. By creating spaces for dialogue, shared learning, and mutual appreciation, these programs continue to be valuable assets in promoting cross-cultural understanding.

V. Promoting Economic Equity:

Economic disparities have perpetuated racial injustice on a global scale. Promoting economic equity becomes an essential component of international efforts for racial justice. Approaches such as affirmative action policies, targeted economic initiatives, and fair employment practices aim to uplift marginalized communities economically. Encouraging diverse representation in leadership positions, private sector partnerships, and corporate responsibility initiatives can also play pivotal roles in addressing economic disparities.

INTERNATIONAL EFFORTS for racial justice provide hope for a future free of discrimination and prejudice. By understanding the historical context, recognizing key global challenges, and acknowledging the roles of international organizations, grassroots movements, education, and economic equity, we can collectively work towards a more inclusive world. Embracing the power of dialogue, empathy, and action, we have the ability to bridge societal divides and promote racial justice on an international scale. Together, we can build a brighter future where all individuals, regardless of their race or ethnicity, can thrive and contribute to a more equitable society.

Building Solidarity Across Borders

One of the key reasons for building solidarity across borders is to address the global challenges that we face today. Challenges such as climate change, poverty, and inequality do not recognize national borders. They require a collective response from all nations and people. Solidarity across borders is crucial in order to mobilize resources, share knowledge, and coordinate efforts to tackle these challenges effectively. By coming together, we can pool our resources and expertise to find innovative solutions that benefit everyone, regardless of their nationality or background.

Another important reason for building solidarity across borders is to foster mutual understanding and empathy between people of different cultures. In a world that is becoming increasingly interconnected, it is essential that we develop a sense of empathy and respect for different cultures and perspectives. Building solidarity across borders helps break down stereotypes, prejudices, and biases that can hinder peaceful coexistence and cooperation. It allows us to appreciate the diversity and richness of human experiences, and to celebrate the commonalities that connect us all.

While building solidarity across borders is undoubtedly a noble goal, it is not without its challenges. One of the main challenges is the existence of social, cultural, and economic barriers that hinder collaboration and understanding. These barriers can manifest in various forms, such as language barriers, cultural differences, and economic disparities. Overcoming these barriers requires genuine efforts to promote cultural exchange, language learning, and economic empowerment. It also requires us to challenge our own biases and prejudices, and to actively seek out opportunities to engage with people from different backgrounds.

To build solidarity across borders, it is essential to create spaces and platforms for dialogue and cooperation. This can be done through initiatives like international conferences, exchange programs, and online platforms that facilitate cross-cultural communication. These spaces provide opportunities for individuals and organizations to come together, share experiences, and collaborate on projects that promote solidarity and mutual understanding. They also allow for the exchange of ideas, knowledge, and best practices, which is crucial for generating innovative solutions and fostering long-term partnerships.

Furthermore, education plays a vital role in building solidarity across borders. Education systems should be designed to promote cultural understanding, empathy, and global citizenship. Schools and universities can integrate global perspectives into their curricula, expose students to diverse cultures and perspectives, and encourage critical thinking and dialogue about global challenges. Educating future generations about the importance of solidarity across borders will help create a more inclusive and compassionate world.

In order to build solidarity across borders, it is also important to address structural inequalities and promote social justice. This requires addressing the root causes of inequalities, such as unfair trade practices, exploitation of resources, and discriminatory policies. Solidarity is not just about showing compassion or empathy; it is about advocating for justice and equality. It is about acknowledging and challenging the systems and structures that perpetuate injustice and inequality, both within and across borders.

In short, building solidarity across borders requires individuals to take action in their everyday lives. It starts with recognizing our own privileges and responsibilities. It means being open-minded, respectful, and inclusive in our interactions with people from different backgrounds. It means supporting organizations and initiatives that promote social justice and human rights. It means speaking up against injustice and advocating for change. Solidarity is not a passive state; it is an active commitment to building a more just and compassionate world. It requires recognizing our shared humanity, fostering mutual understanding, and taking collective action to address global challenges. While there are challenges in building solidarity, such as social, cultural, and economic barriers, they can be overcome through dialogue, education, and addressing structural inequalities. By actively engaging in efforts to build solidarity, we can create a more inclusive, just, and compassionate world for all.

Chapter 15: Environmental Justice and Indigenous Rights

INTERSECTION OF ENVIRONMENTAL and Racial Justice

Environmental justice, first coined in the 1980s, seeks to address the disproportionate exposure of marginalized communities to environmental hazards and the unequal distribution of environmental benefits. It recognizes that certain communities, often economically disadvantaged and racially marginalized, bear a greater burden of pollution and other environmental harm, while enjoying fewer environmental amenities such as clean air and water. The reasons for these disparities are multifaceted, stemming from historical injustices, discriminatory policies, and economic factors.

At its core, environmental justice acknowledges that race is a fundamental factor in determining who bears the brunt of environmental harm. Communities of color are more likely to experience the detrimental effects of industrial pollution, waste disposal sites, and toxic chemicals. These areas, commonly referred to as "sacrifice zones," are characterized by higher rates of asthma, cancer, and other health issues. Moreover, limited access to green spaces or affordable nutritious food further exacerbates health disparities in these communities.

The reasons behind this intersection between environmental and racial injustice are deeply rooted in historical context. Many environmental burdens were deliberately placed in low-income and minority neighborhoods through discriminatory zoning practices and housing segregation. For instance, the practice of redlining in the United States systematically denied access to housing loans and resources to Black and brown communities, making them more vulnerable to living in areas with poor environmental quality. This pattern continues today, perpetuating environmental racism.

The effects of environmental degradation are not limited to physical health. Economic and social opportunities are also impacted. Communities burdened by pollution often face economic disinvestment and limited job opportunities. Environmental hazards can also lead to property devaluation, making it difficult for residents to accumulate wealth and exacerbating socio-economic disparities. This cycle of environmental and racial injustice creates a cycle of poverty and limited upward mobility for marginalized communities.

To address this complexity, it is crucial to consider the intersectionality of multiple dimensions of identity, such as race, gender, immigration status, and socio-economic background. Intersectional analysis unveils the distinct challenges faced by various groups and enables the creation of tailored solutions. It recognizes that multiple forms of discrimination can compound the injustices experienced by individuals. For example, women of color may face unique challenges due to both racial and gender disparities, making it imperative to address these intersecting issues simultaneously.

Environmental and racial justice movements have been working to address these issues and advocate for change. Grassroots organizations, community leaders, and activists have been at the forefront of these efforts, demanding accountability, equitable policies, and community-centered solutions. By amplifying the voices of those most affected, these movements are challenging the status quo and pushing for systemic change.

Mainstream environmental organizations and policymakers are increasingly recognizing the need to integrate racial justice into their work. This entails acknowledging and rectifying the historical legacy of racism within the environmental movement itself. It requires building meaningful partnerships with communities on the frontlines of environmental degradation and involving them in decision-making processes.

Moving towards a more equitable and sustainable future requires a holistic approach that addresses the intersectionality of environmental and racial justice. Policies and initiatives need to be designed with the understanding that progress in one area cannot be achieved without progress in the other. This involves integrating environmental justice considerations into urban planning, transportation, and energy policies. It requires investing in renewable energy infrastructure and ensuring accessibility for all communities. It calls for creating green jobs and prioritizing economic opportunities for marginalized groups. It also necessitates centering the voices and leadership of communities impacted by environmental racism in decision-making processes. It recognizes the disproportionate burden of environmental harm placed on communities of color and highlights the historical and systemic factors contributing to these disparities. By understanding this intersection and working towards integrated solutions, we can strive for a more equitable and sustainable future that ensures environmental well-being for all. Addressing the intersectionality of environmental and racial justice is not only a moral imperative but also a necessary step towards building a just and inclusive society.

Indigenous Perspectives on Land and Resources

These perspectives are rooted in a profound understanding of the interdependence between human beings and the environment, based on principles of sustainability, respect, and reciprocity. In this one, we will explore the rich tapestry of Indigenous knowledge systems, examining how they provide valuable insights into land stewardship and resource management. By delving into these perspectives, we hope to not only increase our understanding of Indigenous cultures but also to highlight the relevance and importance of incorporating Indigenous wisdom into contemporary practices.

Historical Context and Cultural Diversity:

To comprehend Indigenous perspectives on land and resources, it is essential to acknowledge the vast diversity of Indigenous cultures worldwide. From the Inuit of the Arctic to the Maori of New Zealand, each Indigenous community has its distinct heritage, customs, and relationship with their respective lands. Furthermore, understanding the historical context is crucial as colonization has had a profound impact on Indigenous peoples and their traditional practices. Policies of displacement, dispossession, and environmental degradation have caused significant disruption and trauma, leading to the necessity of reclaiming and revitalizing Indigenous perspectives.

Aspects of Indigenous Perspectives:

Indigenous perspectives on land and resources encompass a broad range of interrelated aspects that emphasize the spiritual, ecological, and social dimensions of these connections. Spirituality plays a central role, as Indigenous peoples perceive the land as more than a mere resource; it is viewed as a living entity with inherent value and rights. This viewpoint engenders a profound sense of responsibility towards protecting and honoring the land. Ecological perspectives, on the other hand, stress the importance of sustainable practices that ensure the continued abundance of resources for generations to come. Such practices often involve the use of traditional ecological knowledge, which is passed down through generations and provides valuable insights into sustainable resource management. Additionally, Indigenous perspectives highlight the social dimension, emphasizing the crucial role of community and collective decision-making in maintaining harmony with the land.

Integrating Traditional and Scientific Knowledge:

An essential aspect of Indigenous perspectives on land and resources lies in the integration of traditional and scientific knowledge systems. Indigenous communities have accumulated centuries of empirical knowledge about their local ecosystems, understanding the intricate interdependencies between elements such as plant and animal species, weather patterns, and geographical features. This traditional ecological knowledge holds immense potential for addressing contemporary environmental challenges. By merging Indigenous wisdom with scientific research and methodologies, we can gain a holistic understanding of our environment and develop innovative solutions to sustainability issues.

Challenges and Opportunities:

Despite the valuable contributions of Indigenous perspectives on land and resources, significant challenges and barriers persist. One of the main obstacles is the continued marginalization and exclusion of Indigenous voices from decision-making processes concerning land and resource management. This disconnect not only perpetuates injustices but also hampers the potential for sustainable practices that are crucial in today's context of climate change and ecological degradation. However, there are also promising opportunities for change. Growing recognition of Indigenous rights, increased collaboration between Indigenous communities and non-Indigenous stakeholders, and the implementation of legislation and policies that incorporate Indigenous perspectives are positive steps forward.

INDIGENOUS PERSPECTIVES on land and resources offer profound insights into sustainable land stewardship and resource management. Rooted in values of respect, reciprocity, and interdependence, these perspectives provide a crucial counterbalance to mainstream approaches that often prioritize profit over sustainability. By recognizing and integrating Indigenous knowledge systems, we can foster more equitable and environmentally conscious practices that benefit both present and future generations. Furthermore, it is imperative to address the historical injustices and systemic barriers that have marginalized Indigenous voices, ensuring meaningful participation and partnership in shaping our collective future. Through nurturing a deep appreciation for Indigenous perspectives, we can create a more just, sustainable, and inclusive world.

Chapter 16: Health Disparities and Access to Care

DISPARITIES IN HEALTHCARE for Minority Populations

The existence of disparities in healthcare can be attributed to a complex interplay of socioeconomic, cultural, and systemic factors. Socioeconomic status, for example, plays a significant role in determining an individual's overall health and access to healthcare resources. Minority populations, particularly those from low-income backgrounds, often face barriers to healthcare due to financial limitations, lack of health insurance, and inadequate availability of healthcare facilities in their neighborhoods. As a result, they may delay seeking care or receive substandard treatment.

Cultural factors also contribute to healthcare disparities among minority populations. Language barriers, cultural beliefs, and mistrust in the healthcare system can hinder effective communication and lead to misunderstandings between patients and healthcare providers. Culturally competent care, which values diversity, fosters understanding, and tailors services to individual needs and preferences, is crucial in eliminating these disparities. Healthcare providers need to be aware of and sensitive to the diverse cultural backgrounds of their patients in order to provide equitable care.

Moreover, the systemic factors embedded within our healthcare system perpetuate disparities for minority populations. Structural racism, discrimination, and bias in healthcare delivery and decision-making contribute to unequal treatment and outcomes. Studies have shown that racial and ethnic minorities are often subjected to implicit bias and receive different standards of care compared to their White counterparts, leading to worse health outcomes. Addressing these systemic issues requires systemic changes such as implementing policies that promote diversity in healthcare leadership, increasing representation of minority healthcare providers, and adopting anti-racist practices across healthcare organizations.

The consequences of healthcare disparities for minority populations are profound and far-reaching. These disparities not only result in higher rates of chronic diseases, such as diabetes, hypertension, and obesity, within marginalized communities but also lead to increased mortality rates. Healthcare disparities have a cascading effect on individuals' quality of life, productivity, and overall well-being. Furthermore, they contribute to the perpetuation of social and economic inequalities, as individuals who cannot access proper healthcare are less likely to have equal opportunities for education, employment, and upward mobility.

To address these disparities, a comprehensive and multi-faceted approach is necessary. First and foremost, improving access to quality healthcare services is paramount. This can involve expanding Medicaid, ensuring affordable health insurance options, and increasing the number of primary care providers in underserved areas. Efforts should also be made to eliminate language barriers through interpreter services and providing culturally appropriate care. Additionally, community-based initiatives that raise awareness and educate minority populations on preventive care, healthy lifestyle choices, and the importance of regular check-ups are crucial in reducing disparities.

Another crucial step in eliminating healthcare disparities is addressing the systemic issues that perpetuate unequal treatment. Healthcare organizations should prioritize diversity and inclusion, both in their workforce and in their policies. Recruiting and retaining a diverse healthcare workforce will help create cultural competence and reduce bias in care delivery. Implementing training programs that educate healthcare providers about cultural sensitivity and implicit bias can also make a significant difference. Lastly, it is imperative to invest in research that specifically focuses on understanding, documenting, and addressing healthcare disparities, as well as evaluating the impact of interventions aimed at reducing disparities. The root causes of these disparities are multifaceted, involving socioeconomic, cultural, and systemic factors. The consequences of these inequities are dire, affecting individuals' health outcomes, quality of life, and perpetuating socioeconomic inequalities. To eliminate healthcare disparities, a comprehensive approach that focuses on increasing access to care, cultural competence, and addressing systemic issues is necessary. By working together and implementing evidence-based solutions, we can move towards a more equitable healthcare system that provides quality care to all individuals, regardless of their race or ethnicity.

Promoting Health Equity and Access

It is essential for societies to ensure that individuals, regardless of their socioeconomic background or other marginalizing factors, have equal opportunities to not only access healthcare services but also to achieve optimal health outcomes. The concept of health equity goes beyond mere access to healthcare; it encompasses the elimination of disparities and the provision of fair and just opportunities for individuals to attain their highest level of health. In this book, we will explore the various aspects of promoting health equity and access, aiming to provide a comprehensive understanding of this critical topic.

Understanding Health Equity

To embark on the journey towards promoting health equity, it is crucial to comprehend the concept fully. Health equity refers to the absence of disparities in health outcomes among different groups, such as ethnic populations, socioeconomic classes, or gender orientations. Achieving health equity involves tackling the root causes of inequities and implementing strategies to eliminate barriers to obtaining essential healthcare services. By providing equal opportunities for everyone to maintain good health, we can strive to create a fair and just society.

Identifying Barriers to Health Equity

To address health inequities effectively, it is essential to identify and understand the barriers that hinder individuals from accessing healthcare. These barriers can be multifaceted, ranging from financial constraints and lack of insurance coverage to social determinants of health, such as education, employment, and housing. By recognizing these barriers, policymakers, healthcare providers, and communities can collaboratively design interventions that specifically target and mitigate them, thereby promoting health equity.

Policies for Health Equity and Access

Policy plays a pivotal role in ensuring health equity and access. Governments, alongside public health experts and community leaders, need to establish policy frameworks that are centered on equity and prioritize healthcare for all. Policies should aim to reduce disparities, enhance quality care, and promote prevention and early intervention strategies. By aligning policies with the goal of health equity, we can create an environment that fosters access to healthcare services and helps individuals truly thrive.

Community Engagement and Empowerment

Promoting health equity requires active community engagement and empowerment. Communities possess unique insights and knowledge of their own needs, which should be integrated into healthcare planning and decision-making processes. By fostering partnerships between communities, healthcare providers, and policymakers, we can create a collaborative environment that encourages everyone to take ownership of their health. Empowered communities will be better equipped to identify and implement solutions tailored to their individual contexts, ultimately leading to improved health equity.

Culturally Competent Care

Cultural competence within healthcare settings is fundamental to promoting health equity and access. Providing culturally sensitive care acknowledges the diversity of individuals and the impact that cultural factors have on their health. By integrating cultural understanding and respecting the various beliefs and practices surrounding health, healthcare providers can foster trust and build meaningful relationships with their patients. Culturally competent care not only improves health outcomes but also enhances patient satisfaction and overall health equity.

Health Education and Literacy

Health education and literacy are vital components in promoting health equity and access. Individuals need to be equipped with the knowledge and skills necessary to make informed decisions regarding their health. By providing accessible and culturally appropriate health education programs, we can empower individuals to take charge of their well-being. Furthermore, addressing health literacy disparities among vulnerable groups can significantly improve health outcomes and bridge the gap in health equity.

PROMOTING HEALTH EQUITY and access is a collective responsibility that demands active participation from individuals, communities, healthcare providers, policymakers, and governments. By understanding and addressing the barriers to healthcare access, implementing equitable policies, engaging communities, providing culturally competent care, and promoting health education and literacy, we can gradually bridge the gap in health disparities and strive towards a future where everyone has equal opportunities to live a healthy life. Together, let us embark on this journey to create sustainable change and envision a society where health equity and access are uncompromised realities for all.

Chapter 17: Legal Justice and Advocacy

LEGAL CHALLENGES FACED by Marginalized Communities

Marginalization refers to the social, economic, and legal disadvantages experienced by certain groups, such as racial and ethnic minority communities, LGBTQ+ individuals, women, and persons with disabilities. These challenges can range from discriminatory policing practices to unequal access to justice. This one will explore some of the key legal challenges faced by marginalized communities, the impact they have on the individuals within these communities, and the need for inclusive and equitable legal systems.

Discriminatory Policing and Criminal Justice:

One significant legal challenge faced by marginalized communities is discriminatory policing and the resulting disparities in the criminal justice system. Racial and ethnic minority communities are often subjected to over-policing, racial profiling, and harsher treatment by law enforcement. These practices not only undermine trust in the police and justice system but also perpetuate a cycle of criminalization and marginalization. Similarly, LGBTQ+ individuals may face targeted policing based on their sexual orientation or gender identity, leading to increased harassment, arrest, and discrimination within the criminal justice system. Recognizing and addressing these discriminatory practices is crucial for ensuring the fair and equal treatment of all individuals, regardless of their background.

Access to Justice and Legal Representation:

Another major legal challenge faced by marginalized communities is unequal access to justice. Many individuals within these communities lack the financial resources to afford legal representation, hindering their ability to navigate complex legal systems and protect their rights effectively. Furthermore, racial and ethnic minorities, LGBTQ+ individuals, and other marginalized groups often encounter systemic biases within the legal profession, which may contribute to limited access to competent and culturally sensitive legal services. Addressing this challenge requires the implementation of policies that promote legal aid, community-based legal services, and efforts to increase diversity within the legal profession. Expanding legal resources and ensuring equal access to justice are key steps towards reducing legal inequalities.

Healthcare Disparities and Legal Rights:

Marginalized communities also face legal challenges in accessing adequate healthcare and asserting their rights within the healthcare system. Communities of color and low-income individuals often experience disparities in healthcare access, quality, and outcomes. Legal challenges in healthcare can include discriminatory practices by providers, language barriers, lack of culturally competent care, and limited insurance coverage. Additionally, marginalized communities may encounter challenges in asserting their rights to informed consent, privacy, and non-discrimination within the healthcare system. Legal frameworks that protect the rights of individuals in marginalized communities and promote equitable healthcare access are essential for addressing these challenges.

Housing Discrimination and Segregation:

Housing discrimination and segregation pose significant legal challenges for marginalized communities. Racial and ethnic minority communities, as well as individuals with low incomes, are disproportionately affected by discriminatory housing practices, such as redlining, steering, and unequal access to affordable housing. These practices perpetuate residential segregation, limit access to safe and healthy neighborhoods, and hinder socioeconomic mobility. Legal protections against housing discrimination, as well as efforts to promote fair housing policies and affordable housing initiatives, are critical for ensuring housing equity and dismantling systemic barriers faced by marginalized communities.

Education Inequalities and Discrimination:

Education is widely recognized as a pathway to social and economic mobility. However, marginalized communities often face legal challenges related to educational inequalities and discrimination. Students from racial and ethnic minority communities, low-income neighborhoods, and those with disabilities are more likely to attend under-resourced schools, experience high rates of school discipline, and encounter limited educational opportunities. Furthermore, LGBTQ+ students may face discrimination and harassment in educational settings, impeding their ability to access quality education in a safe and inclusive environment. Legal remedies that address disparities in educational funding, promote inclusive policies, and protect students' rights are crucial for ensuring equitable access to education.

MARGINALIZED COMMUNITIES face numerous legal challenges that compromise their ability to fully participate and thrive in society. Discriminatory policing, unequal access to justice, healthcare disparities, housing discrimination, and educational inequalities are among the key challenges that must be addressed to create more inclusive and equitable legal systems. It is essential for legal professionals, policymakers, and society as a whole to recognize and actively work towards dismantling these legal barriers and ensuring that marginalized communities are afforded the same rights, opportunities, and protections as any other segment of the population. By doing so, we can move closer to a society that respects the dignity and rights of all individuals, regardless of their background or identity.

Advocacy for Legal Reform and Justice

The legal system serves as the foundation of any society, ensuring order and safeguarding the rights and freedoms of its citizens. However, this system is not immune to flaws, biases, and inadequacies. The need for advocacy in legal reform becomes crucial to address these issues and promote an equitable system that truly serves the needs of all.

Understanding the Role of Advocacy:

Advocacy within the legal realm involves raising awareness, initiating change, and influencing policy to improve the justice system's functioning. Advocates for legal reform recognize the potential for a fairer and more just society and work tirelessly to achieve it. By identifying gaps, injustices, and systemic weaknesses, these advocates aim to bridge the divide between the legal system's ideals and its actual delivery of justice. They are the voice for the marginalized, the oppressed, and those seeking redress for their grievances.

Identifying the Need for Legal Reform:

Advocacy for legal reform stems from an ongoing analysis of the existing legal framework. It involves scrutinizing legislation, studying precedents, and monitoring the enforcement of laws to identify areas in need of improvement. Legal reform advocates recognize that laws alone do not guarantee justice. They delve into the challenges faced by communities and individuals, highlighting disproportionate impacts, discriminatory practices, and systemic biases. This data-driven approach enables them to zero in on specific aspects of the legal system that require reform and push for change through evidence-based arguments.

Challenges in the Pursuit of Legal Reform:

Advocacy for legal reform is not without its challenges. The entrenched nature of legal systems, resistance to change, and power imbalances can often impede progress. Advocates face consistent hurdles in convincing policymakers to take action and in garnering support. Additionally, navigating the intricacies of the legal field and effectively communicating complex legal concepts to the public is no easy task. Nevertheless, through perseverance, collaboration, and strategic engagement, advocates can overcome these challenges and pave the way for positive change.

Building Alliances and Collaboration:

Collaboration and alliances are vital in advocacy for legal reform and justice. Advocates come from diverse backgrounds, including legal professionals, academics, grassroots organizations, and affected communities. By pooling their resources, expertise, and networks, these advocates amplify their impact and foster a collective voice. Collaboration helps shape comprehensive reforms that tackle deep-rooted issues, ensuring the legal system becomes more accessible, fair, and inclusive.

Engaging with Policymakers:

To effect meaningful change, advocates must engage with policymakers at all levels. Through dialogue, research, and evidence-based arguments, advocates can present a compelling case for legal reform. Policymakers, though often burdened with competing demands, play a critical role in bringing about necessary changes to the legal system. Advocates must establish fruitful partnerships, both inside and outside the legislative chambers, to influence policy decisions and push for transformative legal reforms that promote a just society.

Public Engagement and Awareness:

Beyond policymakers, advocates need to engage the wider public in their cause. By raising awareness, educating communities, and promoting a wider understanding of legal reform, advocates can cultivate public support for their initiatives. This includes demystifying legal jargon, simplifying concepts, and explaining the impact of legal reform on people's lives. Through public campaigns, social media, town halls, and other outreach activities, advocates can create a groundswell of support, amplifying their message and urging citizens to demand equitable legal practices.

Monitoring and Evaluation:

The work of legal reform advocacy does not end with the implementation of reforms. Continuous monitoring and evaluation of the impact of reforms are essential to ensure they bring about the desired changes. Advocates must work diligently to collect data, assess the effectiveness of reforms, and identify any unintended consequences. This ongoing evaluation ensures that, over time, the legal system evolves and adapts to address emerging challenges, maintain transparency, and safeguard justice for all.

ADVOCACY FOR LEGAL reform and justice lies at the heart of building a more equitable society. It is a multifaceted endeavor that requires a deep understanding of the legal system, collaboration among stakeholders, and strategic engagement with policymakers and the public. By advocating for reform, we can bridge the gap between the ideals of justice and their practical implementation. Together, we can contribute to the evolution of a legal system that ensures equality, protects human rights, and upholds the principles of justice for all.

Chapter 18: Mental Health and Well-being

IMPACT OF RACISM ON Mental Health

It inflicts deep-rooted wounds on individuals and communities, stretching far beyond the realm of its immediate effects. As we delve into the topic of the impact of racism on mental health, it is crucial to acknowledge the unique challenges faced by those affected. This exploration aims to navigate through the intricacies of this relationship, shedding light on the detrimental effects that racism has on individuals, while also advocating for understanding, resilience, and healing.

1. Race, Racism, and Mental Health:

Race is a social construct that categorizes individuals based on shared physical and biological characteristics. However, racism, a byproduct of these racial categorizations, extends beyond mere categorization. Racism encompasses the systemic discrimination, prejudice, and injustice experienced by individuals or groups based on their race. It operates on a spectrum, ranging from overt acts of discrimination to more subtle forms of prejudice or bias.

The mental health of individuals subjected to racism often bears the brunt of its devastating effects. Racism can be considered a chronic stressor, leading to prolonged and cumulative stress experienced at both individual and societal levels. The consequences of this chronic stress can manifest in a range of mental health outcomes, including anxiety, depression, low self-esteem, and other psychological distress.

2. Psychological Distress and Mental Health Morbidity:

Psychological distress resulting from experiences of racism can contribute significantly to mental health morbidity among affected individuals. The stress responses triggered by racism, such as hypervigilance, anticipated discrimination, and internalized racism, can manifest in a variety of psychological symptoms. These symptoms include heightened states of anxiety, persistent feelings of sadness, frustration, helplessness, and an overall sense of being overwhelmed.

Furthermore, marginalized communities, such as ethnic minorities, may face additional stressors, including socioeconomic disadvantages, unequal access to healthcare, and other systemic inequities. These compounding factors can exacerbate psychological distress, perpetuating the cycle of mental health morbidity.

3. Psychological Consequences for Children and Adolescents:

Impaired mental health due to racism is not confined to adults. Children and adolescents who experience racism during their formative years face unique challenges concerning self-identity, social integration, and overall development. Racism at a young age can disrupt their cognitive, emotional, and psychological well-being, limiting their potential and perpetuating intergenerational trauma.

Children subjected to racism may exhibit various behavioral and emotional changes, such as increased aggression, withdrawal, academic underachievement, and low self-esteem. The negative impact of racism on mental health during childhood can have lasting effects, negatively influencing their future mental health outcomes and social trajectories.

4. Coping Mechanisms, Resilience, and Community Support:

Amidst the adverse effects of racism on mental health, it is crucial to highlight the importance of coping mechanisms, resilience, and community support. Many individuals facing racism have developed remarkable resilience, drawing upon their cultural strengths, community resources, and support networks.

Culturally informed coping strategies, such as seeking social support, engaging in cultural practices, or participating in advocacy work, have proven effective in mitigating the impact of racism on mental health. Additionally, community-based interventions and support systems can play an instrumental role in promoting resilience and fostering an environment conducive to healing and growth.

THE IMPACT OF RACISM on mental health is a multifaceted issue, deeply entrenched within our societies. The psychological distress inflicted upon individuals subjected to racism underscores the urgency for comprehensive strategies that address racism at both systemic and individual levels. By fostering understanding, compassion, and resilience, we can strive for a future where mental health disparities due to racism are significantly reduced, creating a more inclusive and equitable society for all.

Promoting Mental Health Awareness and Support

One of the key aspects of promoting mental health awareness is education. Providing accurate information about mental health conditions, their symptoms, and available treatment options helps to dispel myths and misconceptions that often surround these disorders. Education can be delivered through various channels, including schools, workplaces, and community centers. By giving people the knowledge they need, we empower them to recognize the signs of mental health problems in others and themselves, understand the importance of seeking professional help, and maintain a supportive attitude toward individuals who may be struggling.

Unfortunately, mental health issues are still widely stigmatized in many societies. This stigma creates barriers to seeking help, as individuals fear judgment and discrimination. To combat this, efforts to promote mental health awareness must include active destigmatization campaigns. These campaigns can emphasize the fact that mental health disorders are no different from physical health conditions and should be treated with the same level of empathy and understanding. Through sharing personal stories, highlighting successful treatment outcomes, and fostering conversations about mental health, we can gradually break down the stigmatizing beliefs that prevent individuals from seeking support.

In addition to raising awareness and tackling the associated stigma, it is crucial to establish accessible and inclusive support systems for those struggling with their mental health. This can be done by investing in mental health services, such as counseling centers, community-based programs, and hotlines, that cater to individuals across age groups and backgrounds. Provision of affordable or free mental healthcare, particularly in low-income communities, can help make services more accessible to all individuals, regardless of their financial situation.

Furthermore, promoting mental health awareness and support should not be limited to crisis intervention or treatment. It should also encompass comprehensive strategies for mental well-being promotion and prevention. This includes encouraging practices such as mindfulness, self-care, and stress management, which can help individuals build resilience and maintain good mental health. Awareness campaigns can educate people about the importance of self-care and highlight the different ways it can be incorporated into daily routines. By emphasizing preventive measures, we can create an environment that prioritizes mental health as an integral part of overall well-being.

To ensure the success of mental health promotion initiatives, collaboration is vital. This collaboration should involve not only mental health professionals but also policymakers, educators, employers, and the wider community. By working together, different stakeholders can develop comprehensive strategies that address the diverse factors influencing mental health and well-being. Policies can be put in place to support mental health in workplaces, schools, and public spaces. Employers can create supportive environments that prioritize the mental well-being of their employees, while schools can introduce mental health education as part of the curriculum. Community engagement initiatives can foster a sense of belonging and social support, which are crucial protective factors for mental health. By adopting a professional and academic tone while keeping the content approachable and friendly, we can provide a comprehensive understanding of the topic. As we continue to work towards an inclusive and supportive society, it is crucial to prioritize mental health and ensure that individuals feel empowered to seek the help and support they need.

Chapter 19: Art and Activism

ROLE OF ART IN SOCIAL Change

Art has the capacity to bring marginalized voices to the forefront and amplify their experiences. Artists have often used their work to challenge established power structures and bring attention to the struggles of marginalized communities. By giving a voice to those who have been silenced, art has the power to promote empathy and understanding, fostering a more inclusive and just society. Artists like Frida Kahlo, who portrayed her pain and challenges through her self-portraits, or Maya Angelou, who used her poetry to reflect on the African American experience, have been instrumental in paving the way for social change.

Furthermore, art has the ability to challenge societal norms and unveil hidden truths. Artists often push the boundaries of social acceptance and make us question our preconceived notions. Through their work, they challenge the status quo and inspire conversations about important issues. For instance, playwright Lorraine Hansberry explored racial inequality in her iconic work "A Raisin in the Sun," forcing audiences to confront the realities faced by African Americans in the mid-20th century. This play sparked important discussions and contributed to the Civil Rights Movement.

Art also has the power to inspire and mobilize individuals towards social action. Artworks that convey messages of hope, justice, and unity have the potential to galvanize communities and encourage them to strive for a better future. Think of the iconic image of Rosie the Riveter, symbolizing the strength and resilience of women during World War II. This image not only served as propaganda but also empowered women to enter the workforce and challenge traditional gender roles. Similarly, the power of music in social movements such as the anti-war movement or the fight for civil rights cannot be overstated. Songs like Bob Dylan's "Blowin' in the Wind" or Sam Cooke's "A Change is Gonna Come" became anthems of social change, igniting passions and motivating people to fight for justice.

Furthermore, art has the ability to humanize and create connections between individuals. It has the power to evoke empathy and bridge cultural divides. When we are exposed to different forms of artistic expression, we are able to see the world through someone else's eyes and gain a deeper understanding of their experiences. This understanding can break down stereotypes and foster dialogue and cooperation among diverse communities. Similarly, public art installations in urban spaces can transform neglected areas into vibrant communities, promoting local engagement and fostering a sense of pride in one's environment.

In addition to its transformative power on individuals, art can also influence public opinion and policy-making. Artists have played a crucial role in shaping public discourse and influencing political agendas. For example, during the AIDS crisis in the 1980s, artists like Keith Haring used their work to raise awareness and challenge governmental inaction. Through their art, they prompted public discussions and pushed for policy changes that prioritized healthcare and support for those affected by the disease. The role of artists as activists cannot be overstated, as they have the ability to mobilize public opinion and advocate for social justice.

While art alone may not be the solution to all social problems, its role in social change cannot be underestimated. Art has the capacity to challenge, inspire, unite, and transform. It has the power to bring marginalized voices to the forefront, challenge societal norms, mobilize individuals, foster empathy, and influence public opinion. As we navigate the complex challenges facing our societies today, we must recognize and embrace the transformative power of art in creating a more equitable and just world. By supporting and engaging with art, we can contribute to social change and promote a more inclusive and vibrant society for all.

Creativity as a Tool for Resistance

Whether it is against oppressive regimes, discriminatory policies, or deeply rooted prejudices, individuals and communities have sought diverse means to challenge the status quo. One such powerful tool that has emerged is creativity. Creativity as a tool for resistance allows individuals to express themselves, challenge dominant narratives, and imagine alternative possibilities. This essay will explore the multifaceted nature of creativity as a tool for resistance, examining its historical significance, its role in amplifying marginalized voices, and its ability to subvert oppressive structures.

Historical Significance:

Throughout history, humanity has witnessed creativity as a potent means of resistance. Artists, writers, musicians, and performers have used their crafts to challenge prevailing norms and provoke societal change. From the bold brushstrokes of Pablo Picasso's "Guernica," which exposed the horrors of war, to Maya Angelou's poignant poetry that encapsulated the Black experience, creativity has been a catalyst for resistance. Artists like Frida Kahlo, Bob Dylan, and Nina Simone have utilized their mediums to unsettle societal complacency, question authority, and foster a collective consciousness of resistance. By depicting the world in new and unconventional ways, these creative acts enable individuals to begin reflecting on their surroundings and become active agents of change.

Amplifying Marginalized Voices:

Creativity holds a remarkable capacity to amplify the voices of those who have historically been silenced. Marginalized communities have often borne the brunt of oppressive systems, facing discrimination, exclusion, and erasure. However, through creative expression, they can reclaim their narratives and challenge the dominant discourse. By offering alternative perspectives and telling stories that challenge the mainstream narrative, marginalized voices can draw attention to the injustices they face and spark empathy in others. Through mediums such as theater, literature, and visual arts, they can center their experiences, reframe their identities, and ultimately empower themselves in the face of adversity. Creativity, thus, becomes a means to not only resist oppression but also build collective resilience.

Subverting Oppressive Structures:

Resistance often demands challenging the very structures that perpetuate oppression. Creativity allows individuals to disrupt such structures by breaking free from established conventions and norms. Through unconventional approaches, artists can expose and subvert the power dynamics embedded within society. Graffiti on city walls, for example, challenges the notion of who has the authority to define public spaces, transforming them into canvases for dissent. Furthermore, in the digital age, individuals can use various online platforms to challenge oppressive ideologies and structures. Social media, as a tool for resistance, allows marginalized communities to share stories, mobilize support, and create public discourses that can initiate lasting change. In this way, creativity serves as a disruptive force that dismantles the status quo and paves the way for a more just and equitable society.

CREATIVITY POSSESSES immense power as a tool for resistance. Through its historical significance in challenging norms, amplifying marginalized voices, and subverting oppressive structures, creativity has the potential to profoundly impact society. By fostering empathy, dialogue, and critical inquiry, creativity empowers individuals to envision alternative futures and actively work towards their realization. It is through creative acts that we can hope to dismantle oppressive systems and create spaces where voices that have long been silenced can finally be heard. As the world grapples with ongoing injustices, it is crucial to acknowledge and harness the transformative power of creativity as we strive for a more inclusive and equitable future.

Chapter 20: Conclusion

REFLECTIONS ON THE Legacy of Struggle and Resilience

This reflection delves into the intricate relationship between struggle and resilience and aims to shed light on the broad spectrum of challenges individuals and communities have confronted throughout time. By analyzing various historical events, personal stories, and academic research, we will unveil the multifaceted nature of the legacy of struggle and resilience while highlighting its significance for future generations.

Understanding Struggle as Catalyst for Change

Struggle, often regarded as a negative aspect of human life, has consistently played a pivotal role in driving societal progress and personal growth. From the civil rights movements to landmark scientific discoveries, countless examples demonstrate how struggle acts as a catalyst for change. When individuals are faced with formidable challenges, they are compelled to rise above their limitations and overcome adversity, leading to transformative effects rippling across communities and nations. By acknowledging and understanding the transformative potential of struggle, we empower ourselves and future generations to harness its power for positive change.

Resilience as a Fundamental Human Quality

At the core of the human experience lies resilience – the innate ability to adapt and bounce back from adversity. Resilience is not only a personal trait but a collective one, encompassing the spirit of communities and the strength of societies. Examining the history of various cultures and nations, we find countless examples of resilience in the face of hardship – from war-torn regions rebuilding themselves to individuals overcoming personal tragedies. Resilience serves as a guiding light, reminding us of our collective ability to navigate uncertain times and emerge stronger than before.

Historical Perspectives on Struggle and Resilience

Throughout history, we find numerous instances where struggle and resilience have intertwined to shape our understanding of the human experience. From ancient civilizations grappling with conflicts and environmental challenges to modern-day revolutions and socio-political movements, the journey of humanity has been marked by resilience in the face of seemingly insurmountable obstacles. From ancient Rome to the Civil Rights Movement, these narratives provide valuable lessons on how individuals and communities exhibit resilience and confront struggles head-on, leaving a lasting impact on the course of history.

Personal Reflections on Struggle and Resilience

Apart from historical events, personal stories provide powerful glimpses into the enduring human spirit and the nature of struggle and resilience at an individual level. By listening to the narratives of survivors, artists, activists, and everyday individuals, we gain a deeper understanding of how struggles shape lives and, ultimately, legacies. In sharing their stories of personal triumph over adversity, these individuals inspire and remind us of the resilience inherent in all of us, offering valuable lessons for navigating our own challenges.

The Legacy of Struggle and Resilience in Contemporary Times

As we reflect on the legacy of struggle and resilience, it is pertinent to explore how these concepts manifest in our modern world. From global-scale crises such as climate change and pandemics to individual struggles faced in personal and professional lives, contemporary society is ripe with opportunities to cultivate resilience and forge a meaningful legacy. By recognizing the interplay between struggle, resilience, and the collective impact of our actions, we can actively engage in shaping a more inclusive, equitable, and sustainable future.

ULTIMATELY, THE LEGACY of struggle and resilience speaks to the indomitable spirit of humanity – our capacity to face adversity, learn from it, and emerge stronger. By delving into historical contexts, personal narratives, and contemporary challenges, we gain a comprehensive understanding of the transformative power of these concepts. Through reflection and education, we can ensure that the legacy of struggle and resilience remains alive, inspiring future generations to confront challenges head-on and leave their mark on the world.

Looking Towards a More Inclusive Future

Whether it is in the workplace, educational institutions, or society as a whole, the need to create an environment that embraces diversity and promotes equal opportunities has become a pressing issue. While progress has been made, there is still much work to be done to foster a more inclusive future. This book aims to explore various aspects of inclusivity, from understanding its significance to highlighting strategies and initiatives that can help us move towards a more inclusive society.

The Importance of Inclusivity

Inclusivity is not simply a matter of political correctness; it is a fundamental human right. Every individual, regardless of their race, gender, age, ethnicity, religion, or abilities, should be treated with respect and dignity. Inclusive societies are not only fairer but also more innovative and productive. When diverse perspectives are valued and included, it leads to a broader range of ideas, creativity, and problem-solving approaches. Embracing inclusivity also fosters empathy, understanding, and social cohesion, creating a society that is more harmonious and stronger as a whole.

Overcoming Barriers to Inclusivity

While inclusivity is an ideal that we strive for, numerous barriers hinder its achievement. These barriers can be both physical and attitudinal. Physical barriers include inaccessible infrastructure, lack of accommodations for individuals with disabilities, and limitations in technological advancements to bridge gaps. Attitudinal barriers, on the other hand, arise from ingrained biases, stereotypes, unconscious preferences, and discriminatory practices. Overcoming these barriers requires a multi-faceted approach involving education, legislation, and societal transformation. By challenging prejudiced beliefs, adopting inclusive policies, and promoting awareness and understanding, we can break down these barriers and create a more inclusive future.

Promoting Inclusivity in Education

Education plays a vital role in shaping the future. It is the foundation on which societies are built and the vehicle through which values and attitudes are imparted. Therefore, creating inclusive educational institutions is of utmost importance. Inclusive education means providing quality education to all students, regardless of their abilities or backgrounds. It involves adapting teaching methods, curriculum, and learning environments to cater to the diverse needs of students, ensuring that no one is left behind. By embracing inclusive practices, promoting diversity, and fostering a sense of belonging for all students, we can prepare future generations for a more inclusive world.

Cultivating Inclusivity in the Workplace

The workplace is another critical area where inclusivity is crucial. All employees should have an equal opportunity to thrive and contribute. Yet, discrimination, bias, and unequal treatment persist in many workplaces, hindering individuals' professional growth and diminishing the collective potential of organizations. Companies and organizations must commit to creating inclusive work environments by implementing diversity and inclusion strategies, adopting equitable hiring practices, and fostering a culture of respect and acceptance. Embracing diversity in the workforce not only enhances innovation and creativity but also helps organizations build a positive reputation and attract top talent.

Enhancing Inclusive Policies and Legislation

To create lasting change, strong policies and legislation are necessary. Governments, at all levels, have a critical role to play in creating an inclusive future. They can develop and enforce laws that protect individuals from discrimination and promote equal opportunities. Additionally, governments should implement affirmative action programs that address historical and systemic inequalities, ensuring that marginalized communities have equal access to education, employment, healthcare, and social services. By prioritizing inclusivity in policies and legislation, societies can take significant steps towards a fairer, more just future.

Collaboration and Partnerships for Inclusivity

Achieving a more inclusive future requires collaboration among different stakeholders. Governments, civil society organizations, businesses, and individuals must work together towards common goals. Collaboration can take the form of partnerships, joint initiatives, and knowledge-sharing platforms. By leveraging the strengths and resources of different sectors, we can create a more effective and sustainable approach to inclusivity. Collaborative efforts can also enhance cross-cultural understanding, break down silos, and build networks of support, fostering a sense of unity and shared purpose in building an inclusive society.

A MORE INCLUSIVE FUTURE is not merely an aspirational goal; it is an imperative for societal progress and well-being. By prioritizing inclusivity in all aspects of life, from education to the workplace and beyond, we can build a society that appreciates and values diversity, embraces equal opportunities, and fosters mutual respect. It is through collaboration, dialogue, and a collective commitment to inclusivity that we can pave the way for a brighter future, where everyone has the opportunity to thrive and contribute their unique perspectives and talents to the betterment of society as a whole.